ONE NATION, TWO CULTURES

Gertrude Himmelfarb

Alfred A. Knopf   New York   2001

THIS IS A BORZOI BOOK
PUBLISHED BY ALFRED A. KNOPF

Copyright © 1999 by Gertrude Himmelfarb

Published in the United States by Alfred A. Knopf, a division
of Random House, Inc., New York, and simultaneously
in Canada by Random House of Canada Limited, Toronto.
Distributed by Random House, Inc., New York.

www.randomhouse.com

Chapters 1, 3, and 5 are partially based on articles in
The Weekly Standard, Sept. 9, 1996; in *Commentary*, May 1997;
and in *The Public Interest*, Spring 1998.

Library of Congress Cataloging-in-Publication Data
Himmelfarb, Gertrude.
One nation, two cultures / by Gertrude Himmelfarb. — 1st ed.
p.   cm.
ISBN 0-375-40455-4 (alk. paper)
1. Culture. 2. Sociology.   I. Title
HM101.H49 1999
306—dc21   99-18922
CIP

Manufactured in the United States of America
Published November 16, 1999
Second Printing, February 2001

For Robyn and Charles Krauthammer

CONTENTS

PREFACE

"Contemporary history" used to be an oxymoron. History was supposed to be set firmly in the past, recollected in tranquillity, with contemporaries safely dead, passions cooled, and documents neatly stored in archives or awaiting discovery in dusty attics. Like the fifty-year rule governing the release of some official records, courses in history departments stopped well short of the last war or two, the last king or two, certainly the last administration or two (or three or four).

Fernand Braudel, not at all traditional in other respects—one of the foremost practitioners of the *Annaliste* mode of history, which dismisses the ephemera of politics in favor of *la longue durée*, the "deeper realities" of geography, demography, and economy—wrote his monumental work on the Mediterranean in the age of Philip II while confined in a prisoner-of-war camp in Germany during World War II. "All those occurrences," he later wrote, "which poured in upon us from the radio and the newspapers of our enemies, or even the news from London which our clandestine receivers gave us—I had to outdistance, reject, deny them. Down with occurrences, especially vexing ones! I had to believe that history, destiny, was written at a much more profound level."[1]

Those "vexing" occurrences included the bloody battles that eventually led to the defeat of the Nazis and the revelations of one of the most horrendous episodes in human history, the Holocaust.

Other historians, so far from trying to "outdistance, reject, deny" the momentous events of their time, have sought instead to record, analyze, and understand them. (And not only the momentous events but, as the latest genre of "cultural studies" demonstrates, the most trivial and transient ones.) Yet there are lingering traces of doubt and disquiet. Have we forfeited the "long view" that enables us to put the present in perspective? Are we inclined to overestimate the importance of experiences we have personally had and to dramatize events we may have witnessed? Are we unduly impressed by change (a golden age lost or a new world gained) rather than continuity and permanence? And do we find revolutions in every deviation or aberration?

Revolutions present a special difficulty. Historians are wary of the very word. They are even grudging in applying it to political events (was the English Revolution of 1688 a "revolution" or merely a "restoration"?), let alone to social or cultural events. And still more to social or cultural events in their own time. Yet occasionally, very occasionally, they are destined to live through real revolutions. I believe that those of us "of an age" have lived through such a revolution—a revolution in the manners, morals, and mores of society. This does not mean that it has transformed every realm of life, any more than did other revolutions worthy of the name—the industrial revolution last century or the technological revolution more recently. But it has had a profound effect upon our institutions and relationships, private and public.

It has also bequeathed to us, in this postrevolutionary period, a society fragmented and polarized, not only along the familiar lines of class, race, ethnicity, religion, and gender, but along moral and cultural lines that cut across the others. As the implications and consequences of the revolution work themselves out, people have responded with varying degrees of acquiescence and resistance. In their most extreme form, these differences take on the appearance of a moral divide, a "culture war." More often, they express themselves in tensions and dissensions of a lesser order. It is a tribute to the American people and the strength of our traditions and institutions that these disputes have been conducted, for the most part, with civility and sobriety.

Because I myself am leery of the idea of revolution, I have taken special pains to document this one by the hardest kind of evidence, quantified data. Fortunately, one result of this revolution is the availability of just such material. Government agencies and private foundations, research centers in and outside academia, social scientists and pollsters, professional journals, and even the daily newspapers produce a variety of statistics, surveys, analyses, polls, charts, graphs, and tables that are the envy of historians working on more remote periods of the past. I do not, to be sure, subscribe to the dictum, attributed to the British scientist Lord Kelvin, etched over a window in the Social Science building of my alma mater, the University of Chicago: "When you cannot measure, your knowledge is meager and unsatisfactory." I believe there are other sources of knowledge that are sometimes more compelling than numbers: philosophy, history, literature, tradition, religion, common sense. I am also wary of quantification when it is represented as the sole or highest form of historical evidence, particularly for periods of the past when it is sparse and highly selective, and when whatever statistics happen to exist are permitted to determine the subjects that the historian deems worthy of attention. But for the study of contemporary affairs, where such information is both plentiful and pertinent, these reservations do not hold. Statistics can be faulty and polls deceptive, and neither should be taken too literally or precisely. But used in conjunction with other kinds of evidence ("impressionistic," "literary," or "theoretical," as quantifiers say disparagingly), they have been invaluable in establishing some hard facts and correcting some common misconceptions.

I am grateful, therefore, to those who have helped me find my way among these once unfamiliar sources: my friends Karlyn Bowman and Charles Murray, both of the American Enterprise Institute, John DiIulio of Princeton University, and James Q. Wilson of the University of California at Los Angeles, who have so generously given me of their time and formidable knowledge; my research assistant, Helen Boutrous, who has been so assiduous in retrieving articles from obscure journals and dredging up reports from the deepest entrails of the Government Printing Office and the Internet; and the many scholars who have graciously responded to my queries about subjects in their special areas of expertise. And once again, as with more than half-a-dozen of my earlier books, I have had the unfailing encouragement of my editor, a gentleman-publisher of the old school, Ashbel Green.

My greatest debt, now as always, is to my husband, Irving Kristol. That he is a constant source of intellectual stimulation goes without saying. Perhaps more relevant on this occasion is his steadfast character. It may be that I am all the more sensitive to the condition of the culture today, its volatility and infirmity, because it is in contrast to his constancy and vitality, which have sustained me and our family for these very many years.

ONE NATION,
TWO CULTURES

CHAPTER I
A HISTORICAL PROLOGUE:
THE "VICES OF LEVITY" AND THE
"DISEASES OF DEMOCRACY"

In *The Wealth of Nations*, Adam Smith described the "two different schemes or systems of morality" that prevail in all civilized societies.

> In every civilized society, in every society where the distinction of ranks has once been completely established, there have been always two different schemes or systems of morality current at the same time; of which the one may be called the strict or austere; the other the liberal, or, if you will, the loose system. The former is generally admired and revered by the common people: the latter is commonly more esteemed and adopted by what are called people of fashion.

The liberal or loose system is prone to the "vices of levity"—"luxury, wanton and even disorderly mirth, the pursuit of pleasure to some degree of intemperance, the breach of chastity, at least in one of the two sexes, etc." Among the "people of fashion," these vices are treated indulgently. The "common people," on the other hand, committed to the strict or austere system, regard such vices, for themselves at any rate, with "the utmost abhorrence and detestation," because they—or at least "the wiser and better sort" of them—know that these vices are almost always ruinous to them. Whereas the rich can sustain years of disorder and extravagance—indeed, regard the liberty to do so without incurring any censure or reproach as one of the privileges of their rank—the people know that a single week's dissipation can undo a poor workman forever. This is why, Smith explained, religious sects generally arise and flourish among the common people, for these sects preach that system of morality upon which their welfare depends.[1]

Much of the social history of modern times can be written in terms of the rise and fall, the permutations and combinations, of these two systems. Smith knew, of course, that these "systems" are just that—prescriptive or normative standards against which people are judged but which they often violate in practice. He had no illusions about the actual behavior of either class; he did not think that all "people of fashion" indulged in these "vices of levity," nor that all the "common people," even the "wiser and better" of them, were paragons of virtue. But he did assume that different social conditions found their reflection in different moral principles and religious institutions. Thus the upper classes were well served by a lenient established church, while the lower classes were drawn to the austere dissenting sects.*

Smith was writing in the wake of the Wesleyan revival earlier in the century, which had brought both religion and an austere system of morality to a considerable part of the lower classes. What he did not anticipate was that Wesleyanism would shortly spread to the middle classes in the form of Evangelical-

---

*But perhaps too austere, Smith suspected. Himself a man not of "fashion" but of the enlightenment, he thought that the morals of the sects were "disagreeably rigorous and unsocial," and that the government would be well advised to dispel their "melancholy and gloomy humour" by encouraging decent "public diversions" in the form of art, music, dancing, poetry, and plays.[2]

ism and would inspire a "Moral Reformation" movement that before long would pervade all classes. In 1787 (eleven years after the publication of *The Wealth of Nations* and three years before Smith's death), that movement received the imprimatur of George III in a royal proclamation for the "Encouragement of Piety and Virtue, and for the Preventing and Punishing of Vice, Profaneness, and Immorality." The proclamation was followed by the formation of a society for this purpose, which took its place among the many other societies devoted to such worthy causes as the "Preservation of Public Morals," the "Suppression of Public Lewdness," and the "External Observance of the Lord's Day"—all of which were directed at least as much to the middle and even upper classes as to the lower classes. When Hannah More, a convert to Evangelicalism and an enthusiastic proponent of moral reformation, called upon the rich to give up their vices (the theater was her particular bête noire), she urged them to do so not only for their own salvation but to set an example to the poor, inspiring them to give up *their* habitual vices (drink, most notably).

By the middle of the nineteenth century, that austere ethos, which we now know as "Victorianism," had become the official credo, as it were, of the whole country.* Work, thrift, temperance, fidelity, self-reliance, self-discipline, cleanliness, godliness—these were the preeminent Victorian virtues, almost universally accepted as such even when they were violated in practice.[4] The "liberal or loose system of morality" continued to exist, to be sure, on the fringes of society, among the rakish

---

*Literally the official credo. In 1862, Queen Victoria, in a proclamation echoing that of her grandfather, declared it her duty "to maintain and augment the service of Almighty God, as also to discourage and suppress all vice, profane practice, debauchery and immorality," in furtherance of which she prohibited the playing of cards or other games on the Lord's Day and bade her subjects "to attend, with decency and reverence, at Divine Service."[3]

elements of the aristocracy and the "unrespectable" poor. But even among them, it became less prominent in the course of time, as more of the "idle" aristocracy were absorbed into the industrial and commercial world, and as more of the "indolent" poor were assimilated into the working classes.

At the end of the nineteenth century the loose system was rehabilitated by a small group of bohemians who deliberately and ostentatiously cultivated the "vices of levity"—vices far more "decadent" (a term they themselves used) than anything Smith had envisaged. Most of the members of this fin de siècle cult survived these vices, as the rich had survived them in Smith's time. If Oscar Wilde was ruined by them, it was not because, like the unfortunate laborer a century earlier, his dissipation meant starvation, but because he recklessly provoked a legal suit that led to public exposure and punishment. A later generation of bohemians, the Bloomsbury set, was more discreet in public, although not at all in private. Like their fin de siècle predecessors, this small, self-contained group of artists and writers assumed for themselves a moral license they did not extend to society as a whole. ("Immoralists," John Maynard Keynes, who was one of them, candidly called them.)[5] Repudiating Victorian morality, many of them were as contemptuous of the working classes who adhered to that morality as of the bourgeoisie who celebrated it. But they had no desire to liberate either of these classes from a morality that served them, the intellectual elite, so well, providing the goods and services they needed for their own "higher" callings.* In this respect the

---

*Two days after the armistice that brought World War I to an end, when most Englishmen were rejoicing that the bloodshed was finally over, Virginia Woolf wrote to her sister: "The London poor, half drunk and very sentimental or completely stolid with their hideous voices and clothes and bad teeth, make one doubt whether any decent life will ever be possible."[6] In the same spirit she described James Joyce as a pretentious workingman or, at best, "a queasy undergraduate

English bohemians of the early twentieth century resembled the "people of fashion" of Smith's day, who enjoyed a privileged morality (or amorality) not shared by the common people and who indulged their vices with impunity and without reproach— certainly without self-reproach.

When Smith said that those two systems of morality prevail in "every civilized society," he was careful to specify that this meant "every society where the distinction of ranks has once been completely established." There was one civilized society, however, where that distinction was not established and where those two systems of morality did not prevail—not then, at any rate. In this respect, America, even then, was an "exceptional country." It had not abandoned the Puritanism that was its heritage; it had not undergone a cultural, still less a political, Restoration, like that of England. If the rich indulged in "vices of levity," they were regarded as vices, not as privileges of rank. Perhaps this is why the Founders did not think it necessary to introduce the idea of virtue into the Constitution, or to give the government any positive role in promoting the morals of the citizenry. They simply assumed that there was, as the *Federalist Papers* put it, "sufficient virtue" in the people to sustain self-government.[8] Colonial and early republican America was "Victorian" *avant la lettre*.

What is extraordinary is that "Victorianism," in principle at least, survived throughout the following century, in spite of a host of circumstances that might have militated against it: a civil war that very nearly destroyed the unity and morale of the nation, successive waves of immigration bringing in people

---

scratching his pimples." *Ulysses*, she said, was "an illiterate, underbred book . . . , the book of a self taught working man, and we all know how distressing they are, how egotistic, insistent, raw, striking, and ultimately nauseating."[7]

from very different cultures and societies, the opening up of the frontier and the expansion into territories that were remote from the culture of the founding colonies, the social tensions of the Reconstruction era and the Gilded Age—all of this accompanied by momentous changes in industry, commerce, transportation, and urbanization. English visitors to the United States—Charles Dickens, Harriet Martineau, Frances Trollope, Matthew Arnold—were disturbed by the curious combination of individualism and egalitarianism which seemed so typically American and encouraged such disagreeable habits as spitting and bragging. But they were also impressed by the moral quality of the domestic lives of Americans and by the responsible nature of their public discourse and activities. Even Arnold, for whom the United States had always represented the height of vulgarity and philistinism—he quoted another traveler who said that "there is no country that called itself civilised where one would not rather live than in America, except Russia"[9]—was impressed by the social equality of the country, the lack of class distinctions in spite of great inequalities of wealth. (It was the example of America that induced him, upon his return to England, to advocate the abolition of all titles.)*

It is also remarkable that in spite of the tumultuous conditions of nineteenth-century America, the Victorian ethos of the new country had so much in common with that of the old. In the United States as in England, that ethos was shared by the working as well as middle classes. As in England, too, it gradu-

---

* It is curious to find that Americans, who had thought of Arnold as the epitome of urbanity, sophistication, and aristocratic demeanor, were more disappointed in him than he was in them. They found him coarse, even "common," in manner and appearance, pretentious and patronizing, materialistic and greedy. Apocryphal stories circulated that he demanded an honorarium before receiving an honorary degree. Walt Whitman, perhaps repaying Arnold for being dismissive of his *Leaves of Grass*, pronounced him "the perfect Philistine."[10]

ally became secularized in the course of the century, without, however, losing its vigor or authority. Even the cultural rebels—abolitionists, feminists, radicals—professed a commitment to Victorian values, often invoking the authority of John Stuart Mill, Thomas Carlyle, and Matthew Arnold. One historian speaks of the relationship between these eminent Victorians and the American representatives of the "Genteel Tradition" as the "Victorian Connection."[11] Another explains that Victorianism was "experienced more intensely in the United States than in Victoria's homeland," because there was no aristocratic tradition against which the middle classes had to contend.[12] Yet another attributes the dominance of this culture to the "plethora of bylaws, ordinances, statutes, and common law restrictions regulating nearly every aspect of early American economy and society"[13]—laws that reflected and reinforced the manners and morals, habits and social sanctions, that defined the Victorian ethos.

It was against this Victorianism that a generation of American bohemians (again, like the Bloomsbury set in England) rebelled after the turn of the century. "Everybody knows," a distinguished historian has written, "that at some point in the twentieth century America went through a cultural revolution."[14] Writing in 1959, on the very eve of what we now know as "the cultural revolution," Henry May was referring not to the revolution of the 1960s but to that which started shortly before the First World War and came to fruition in the 1920s. Echoing Virginia Woolf's description of the spirit animating Bloomsbury in its inception—"everything was going to be new; everything was going to be different; everything was on trial"[15]—May describes its American counterpart: "The twenties were the period of beginnings, the time when social scientists and psychologists announced a brave new world, when technological accomplishment fixed a new image of America in the eyes of jealous

Europe, when Henry L. Mencken created a new language to castigate the bourgeoisie, and the Young Intellectuals found new reasons for rejecting the whole of American culture."[16]

America's "Young Intellectuals," however, were only superficially similar to England's Bloomsbury. If they were hostile to what Mencken called the "booboisie," they were not at all indifferent to, let alone contemptuous of, the working classes. On the contrary, most of them (with the notable exception of Mencken) were staunchly progressive, reform-minded, even socialistic in their political views. Nor was their sexual revolution at all like that of their English cousins. Unlike Bloomsbury, which was flagrantly promiscuous (one needs a diagram to follow the complicated affairs—simultaneous and successive, homosexual and heterosexual—of its members), their counterparts in Greenwich Village were relatively reserved in their bohemianism. Walt Whitman, their hero, is celebrated today as a homosexual; then, he was known and admired as a romantic and a democrat. Nor was the "Flapper Set," as Mencken baptized it—"lovely and expensive and about nineteen," F. Scott Fitzgerald described one of them[17]—as outrageous as an older generation thought. Their indulgences consisted of kissing, smoking, drinking, partying, and petting in automobiles ("necking," as it was called). In *This Side of Paradise*, published in 1920, Fitzgerald observed: "None of the Victorian mothers—and most of the mothers were Victorian—had any idea how casually their daughters were accustomed to be kissed."[18] Kissed!—Bloomsbury would have been amused by so quaint a notion of liberation. (The word was not a euphemism, as we might now suppose.)

Compared with the Victorian period that preceded it, the early twentieth century may well seem to have inaugurated, as one historian put it, "the first sexual revolution."[19] The First World War had a dissolvent effect upon conventional belief and behavior. But even before that, the increasing secularization and urbanization of society, the employment of women in large numbers and diverse occupations, the suffragette movement (culminating in the acquisition of the vote after the war), the widespread practice and, no less important, the candid discussion of contraception, the advent of automobiles providing an unprecedented degree of mobility and freedom—all of these led to a relaxation of traditional social and sexual mores. Even the "social hygiene" movement, which was intended to improve morals by obliging men to adhere to the same standard as women and exposing the dangers of venereal disease, had the unintended result of liberating both men and women from their customary roles and attitudes. A widely quoted article by Agnes Repplier in the *Atlantic Monthly* in 1914, "The Repeal of Reticence," deplored the loss of parental authority and the moral laxity that came from this loosening of standards and conventions.

The "first sexual revolution," however, was less subversive than the label suggests. In their case study of "Middletown" in the mid-twenties, Robert and Helen Lynd noted that the higher rate of divorce and greater use of contraception were not accompanied by significantly more permissive sexual attitudes or behavior. Among the young, there may have been some "tentative relaxing" of the heavy taboo against sexual relations between unmarried persons, but in general that taboo "is as strong today as in the county-seat of forty years ago."[20] Middletown (and, one may presume, similar towns throughout the country) adapted itself more tentatively and moderately to changing material and social conditions than some contemporaries at the time, or later historians, have supposed.

Whatever cultural revolution America experienced in the 1920s or before, it was a faint foreshadow of what was to follow. In 1942, the economist Joseph Schumpeter located the source of the revolution in capitalism itself. In *Capitalism, Socialism, and Democracy*, he described the "species" or "class" of intellectuals who flaunted their contempt for the capitalist society in which they flourished, indulged their sense of moral superiority over the materialistic culture that nurtured them, and exploited the freedom granted to them by the laws and institutions of the bourgeois society they reviled. The "sociology of the intellectual," however, was only a digression in Schumpeter's thesis. The heart of it was the inherent vulnerability, the fatal flaw, of capitalism itself. The rationalistic, entrepreneurial spirit that ensured capitalism's economic success, Schumpeter argued, had the unwitting effect of undermining both the bourgeois ethos and the traditional institutions that sustained it. Thus capitalism was constantly being subverted by the very process of "creative destruction" that provided its economic dynamic. Eventually, Schumpeter predicted, capitalism itself would be destroyed, aided and abetted by its own intellectuals.

> In breaking down the pre-capitalist framework of society, capitalism thus broke down not only barriers that impeded its progress but also flying buttresses that prevented its collapse. . . . Capitalism creates a critical frame of mind which, after having destroyed the moral authority of so many other institutions, in the end turns against its own; the bourgeois finds to his amazement that the rationalist attitude does not stop at the credentials of kings and popes but goes on to attack private property and the whole scheme of bourgeois values.[21]*

---

*A century earlier, John Stuart Mill pointed to a similar flaw in capitalism. Convinced that the competitive and acquisitive instincts released by a "progressive economy" would be conducive to an unseemly materialism and hedonism, he proposed restraining the economy by deliberately keeping it in a "stationary state."[22] The Victorians rejected this solution for the good reason that it would have impeded not only materialism and hedonism but also the industrial and technological advances that were making life more livable for masses of people. Secure in their own values, they were confident that society could withstand the challenges posed by the new economy.

This prediction has not been entirely borne out. Capitalism continues to flourish, and over a greater expanse of the world than ever before. But the process of "creative destruction" has taken its toll on the moral life of society. Indeed, it has proved to be both more creative and more destructive than Schumpeter could have anticipated. Capitalism has survived, it would seem, but at the expense of the bourgeois ethos that originally inspired it and that long sustained it.

In the aftermath of the Second World War, the Western world, and the United States most dramatically, began to experience the benefits of an open society and a thriving economy: a release from the pressures of depression and war, an affluence that permitted an unprecedented expansion and dispersion of material goods, an extension of higher education to classes that had been deprived of it, and a host of scientific and technological innovations that prolonged, improved, enriched, and energized life for most people.

Today, it is common to hear the fifties described as a period of sexual repression and patriarchal oppression, bleak conformism and quiet desperation. Yet it was in this period (as Theodore Roszak, who coined the term "counterculture," pointed out) that the revolutionaries of the sixties were nurtured. So far from being repressed or oppressed, they had been brought up by doting parents following the permissive prescriptions of Dr. Benjamin Spock, whose books on child care were the bible of the generation. (The first of these perennial bestsellers was published in 1946; others followed in the fifties.) As young adults they enjoyed the privilege of attending the colleges that flourished in that decade, thanks in part to the G.I. Bill of Rights and the massive infusion of government funds. (The college population more than doubled between 1950 and 1964.) It was there that they found the intellectual stimulus to challenge the dominant culture, as well as a supportive peer culture. Some identified themselves with the "Beatniks," the followers of Jack Kerouac and Allen Ginsberg, who were the vanguard of the rebellion. Others learned their tactics of dissent in the anti-McCarthy movement that continued to thrive even after the senator himself was censured in 1954, and in the antinuclear campaign that developed shortly afterward. (SANE was founded in 1957, the year of Joseph McCarthy's death.) Still others were inspired by the artistic vanguard that made a hero of Jackson Pollock and a figure of fun of Norman Rockwell.

Moreover, they, and their parents, were prepared for the sexual revolution by the Freudianism that was so pervasive and influential in the postwar generation, inspiring prolonged periods of therapy for those who could afford it and a vast literature for those who could not. The Kinsey Report on male sexuality was published in 1948 and that on female sexuality in 1953, Herbert Marcuse's *Eros and Civilization* appeared in 1955, and a host of how-to manuals made the best-seller lists by revealing the techniques for sexual liberation and fulfillment. In 1956, the Harvard sociologist Pitirim Sorokin published *The American Sex Revolution,* deploring, with all the passion of a latter-day evangelical preacher, the "sexualization of American culture" and "sham-Nietzschean amorality" that were engulfing the country. "What used to be considered morally reprehensible is now recommended as a positive value; what was once called demoralization is now styled moral progress and a new freedom."[23]

Even the civil rights movement had its dramatic beginnings in the fifties with Rosa Parks's refusal, in December 1955, to give up her seat on a bus in Montgomery, Alabama. It was then that Martin Luther King emerged to national prominence by leading, and winning, the boycott against the segregated bus system in that city. In 1957 he created the Southern Christian Leadership Conference, which carried his message of nonviolent resistance together with the desegregation campaign throughout the South and, finally, the nation. When enthusiasts for the sixties pride themselves on doing away with the bad old days of the fifties—the benighted age of *Leave It to Beaver*—it is well to remember that there was much going on outside of the Cleaver household. If the sixties were a reaction to the fifties, the fifties were also a prelude to the sixties.

Only, however, a prelude, for all of these developments, and others as well, were so intensified and accelerated in the sixties and the following decades that they appeared at the time (and in retrospect) as a genuine moral and cultural revolution—a revolution that confirmed Schumpeter's predictions about the ambiguous effects of material progress. As society became more open and the economy more affluent, morality and culture were liberalized and democratized. The "loose system of morality," bursting out of the class binds that had constrained it, was made available to everyone. To be sure, most people, most of the time, chose not to avail themselves of it. But it was there potentially, a siren call to "levity" and liberation. For the common people, it brought with it many virtues, including the great one of no longer being identified as the "common people." But it was also fraught with temptations and vices that were all the more difficult to resist because they came with the imprimatur of their social and intellectual betters.

The 1960s brought to a head the "cultural contradictions of capitalism," in Daniel Bell's memorable phrase: the contradictions inherent in an economy that requires, for its effective functioning, such moral restraints as self-discipline and deferred gratification, but at the same time stimulates a hedonism and self-indulgence impatient of all restraints.[24] One of these "contradictions" was the manipulation and exploitation of capitalism by those who professed to despise it. Like Schumpeter's "intellectuals," many "hippies" proved to be skillful at commercializing their own talents and converting their countercultural activities into profitable enterprises. Thus, entire industries arose devoted to pseudo-folk art and attire, "head shops" specializing in drug paraphernalia and herb shops in "nature remedies," and avant-garde galleries and theaters that were patronized and often subsidized by the bourgeois capitalists who were being satirized. In 1965, Lionel Trilling took the measure of the "adversary culture," as he called it. Propagated initially by modernist writers and artists, it had a deliberately "adversary intention," an "actually subversive intention," towards the traditional bourgeois culture. In the 1960s, however, it took a form that was quantitatively as well as qualitatively unique, for it now characterized not a small group but an entire class, a class that was most conspicuous in the universities but that spilled over into society at large—indeed, into the very middle class that was its ostensible enemy. Although it did not dominate the middle class, Trilling observed, it "detached a considerable force from the main body of the enemy and . . . captivated its allegiance."[25]

Within only a few years of that prescient comment, Trilling's "adversary culture" developed into the "counterculture," embracing far more people than he anticipated at the time. It even surpassed the expectations of Theodore Roszak, who, in 1968, in an article "Youth and the Great Refusal" in *The Nation*, introduced and defined this new phenomenon: "The counter culture is the embryonic cultural base of New Left politics, the effort to discover new types of community, new family patterns, new sexual mores, new kinds of livelihood, new aesthetic forms, new personal identities on the far side of power politics, the bourgeois home, and the Protestant work ethic."[26] The term gained wide circulation when the essay was reprinted two years later in Roszak's *The Making of a Counter Culture*. But even then he underestimated the appeal of the counterculture, for he confined it to "a strict minority of the young and a handful of their adult mentors"; in a few generations, he speculated, their heirs might "transform this disoriented civilization of ours into something a human being can identify as home."[27]

. . .

In fact, the counterculture progressed far more rapidly and widely than even its most enthusiastic supporters predicted, for it proved to be nothing less than a cultural revolution. And this revolution was magnified by other concurrent ones: a racial revolution (inspired by the civil rights movement); a sexual revolution (abetted by the birth-control pill and feminism); a technological revolution (of which television was a notable by-product); a demographic revolution (producing a generation of baby-boomers and a powerful peer culture); a political revolution (precipitated by the Vietnam War); an economic revolution (ushering in the Great Society and the expansion of the welfare state); and what might be called a psychological revolution (the "culture of narcissism," as Christopher Lasch dubbed it).[28]* Each was momentous in itself and together they fed upon each other, fostering a growing disaffection with established institutions and authorities and a rejection of conventional modes of thought and behavior.

Blacks and women celebrate this period as the beginning of their liberation, their admission into a world of rights, liberties, and opportunities from which they had been so unjustly excluded. The celebration is warranted and the liberation much appreciated. But it was not long before anomalies emerged—the "cultural contradictions of liberation," one might say. Some women found that they were liberated from the home in more than one sense. The rise in the employment rate for women paralleled a rise in the divorce and single-parenthood rates. Many

*Perhaps because he was writing in the late 1970s at a time of economic stagnation, Lasch associated the culture of narcissism with an "age of diminishing expectations," as his subtitle put it. In fact, that culture flourished even more in the age of rising expectations of the eighties and nineties.

women, having gained entry into the workplace, lost their secure place in the marital home. And having become "gainfully employed" (as economists understand that term), they were often reduced to the condition of poverty that accompanies divorce and single-parenthood.

For blacks the situation turned out to be equally anomalous. Freed from the degrading conditions of segregation and discrimination, most blacks, including working-class blacks, came to enjoy a higher standard of living, more varied and desirable jobs, and better education and housing. But others, in this "post–civil rights era," as the black economist Glenn Loury calls it, found themselves in a "moral quandary," dependent upon a government-subsidized welfare system that provided for their basic needs but put them in the unfortunate condition of victimhood and dependency—a condition that might be rectified, Loury suggests, by utilizing those resources within their own community that promote a sense of self-confidence and "self-help."[29]

Thus the counterculture, intended to liberate everyone from the stultifying influence of "bourgeois values," also liberated a good many people from those values—virtues, as they were once called—that had a stabilizing, socializing, and moralizing effect on society. It is no accident, as Marxists used to say, that the rapid acceleration of crime, out-of-wedlock births, and welfare dependency started at just the time that the counterculture got under way.

It is a much-debated question whether we could have enjoyed the good without the bad, the desirable effects of the cultural revolution without the undesirable. Revolutions, it is well known, develop a momentum of their own, often escalating beyond their original aims and ending up by consuming both their parents and their children. And the conjunction of revolutions, such as occurred in the 1960s, made it probable that the unintended consequences would eventually overwhelm the intended ones. Thus the beneficial results of the civil rights movement were partially—fortunately only partially—negated by two other developments that coincided with it: the cultural revolution that denigrated precisely those virtues (work, thrift, temperance, self-discipline) that are conducive to economic improvement and social mobility; and the Great Society, which was meant to facilitate the entry of minorities into the open society of opportunity and self-fulfillment, but all too often drew them into a closed society of chronic dependency.

The Vietnam War gave the sixties a special salience in the United States. But the cultural revolution was not confined to this country; on the contrary, it emerged at the same time in Western nations that did not go through the traumatizing experience of that war.[30] If some of the effects of this revolution—single-parenthood or out-of-wedlock births, for example—do not occupy Europeans as much as they do Americans (with the exception of the English, who are much troubled by them), this may reflect the ethos of those countries more than the objective conditions.* And if Americans are acutely aware of these conditions, if we perceive them as serious problems, it is because we have traditionally prided ourselves on being not only the most democratic nation but also the most moral one—moral because democratic.

Long before the founding of the American republic, Montesquieu explained that "virtue" is the distinctive characteristic of a republic, as "honor" is of a monarchy and "moderation" of an aristocracy. If Europeans do not share our "obsession," as they say, with morality, dismissing it disparagingly as "moralistic," it is perhaps because their ethos still has lingering traces of

---

* Out-of-wedlock births ratios, for example, between 1960 and 1990 rose from 5 percent to 28 percent in the United States and the United Kingdom; from 4 percent to 24 percent in Canada; from 6 percent to 30 percent in France; from 8 percent to 46 percent in Denmark; and from 11 percent to 47 percent in Sweden. (Most of these figures are considerably larger today.[31])

their monarchic and aristocratic heritage—those vestiges of class, birth, and privilege that are congenial to a "loose" system of morality. Americans, having been spared that legacy and having relied from the beginning upon character as the test of merit and self-discipline as the precondition of self-government, still pay homage to the idea of "republican virtue."

Two centuries ago, the Founding Fathers addressed what was then the most serious issue confronting the new nation. A famous passage in the *Federalist Papers* looks to the Constitution for "a republican remedy for the diseases most incident to republican government."[32] The diseases the Founding Fathers had in mind were "the mischiefs of faction": the pursuit of special interests to the detriment of the general interest. To counteract those diseases, they proposed the system of federalism and the separation of powers.

Later generations have been less concerned with the diseases incident to republican government than with those incident to democratic society—poverty, racism, unemployment, inequality. More recently we have confronted yet other species of diseases, moral and cultural: the collapse of ethical principles and habits, the loss of respect for authorities and institutions, the breakdown of the family, the decline of civility, the vulgarization of high culture, and the degradation of popular culture. In poll after poll, even at the height of economic prosperity, a great majority of the American people (as many as two-thirds to three-quarters) identify "moral decay" or "moral decline" as one of the major problems, often *the* major problem, confronting the country.[33]*

*This sense of moral decline is not belied by the fact that people often exempt themselves and those closest to them from it. The "I'm O.K., you're not" attitude is known as the "optimism gap." According to one survey, two-thirds of the people "feel good" about their own

In its most virulent form this "decay" manifests itself in the "moral statistics" (as the Victorians called them—"social pathology," we would say) of crime, violence, out-of-wedlock births, teenage pregnancy, child abuse, drug addiction, alcoholism, illiteracy, promiscuity, welfare dependency. Some of these statistics have improved in the last few years and there are hopeful signs for the future. The most dramatic decline has been in crime. From 1990 to 1997, serious crimes (robbery, larceny, automobile thefts) fell from 58 per thousand to 49; violent crimes from 7.3 to 6.1; homicides from 9.4 per 100,000 to 6.8; the black homicide rate from 38 per 100,000 to 28.5 (in 1996); and homicides by young teenagers (fourteen- to seventeen-year-olds) from 30.2 per 100,000 (in 1993) to 16.5 (in 1997).[35] In cities with populations of over a million, homicides fell from 35.5 per 100,000 in 1991 to 20.3 in 1997—the lowest rate in two decades. In New York City the change has been most palpable, on subways, in the streets, and in homes; again, the most remarkable figures concern homicides: 2,262 in 1990, 620 in 1998.[36]

Next to crime, the welfare situation has been most promising. The number of people on welfare fell by more than a third, from 14.1 million in January 1993 to 7.6 million in December 1998.[37] Less dramatic but still significant declines are registered in out-of-wedlock births (from 47 per thousand unmarried women in 1994 to 44 in 1997);[38] teenage births (from 62.9 per thousand in 1991 to 52.3 in 1997);[39] the sexual activity of fifteen- to nineteen-year-old girls (from 55 percent in 1990 to 50 percent in 1995), and of boys (from 60.4 percent in 1988 to 55.2 percent in 1995);[40] divorces (from 4.7 per thousand population in 1990

---

communities, but only one-third have good feelings about America in general.[34] This resembles the "self-esteem" syndrome which induces people to have a higher opinion of their own abilities than others have of them (or than is warranted by objective measures). The optimism gap, like the spurious self-esteem, is a kind of cognitive dissonance, a reluctance to confront reality.

to 3.9 in 1997);[41] and abortions (from 27.4 per thousand women [eighteen- to forty-four-year-olds] in 1990 to 22.9 in 1996).[42]

A pessimist, it has been said, cannot take yes for an answer. But even an inveterate pessimist must be heartened by these developments—and heartened not only by the existential improvement in the lives of Americans as reflected in these statistics, but also by the probable causes for that improvement. The early 1990s saw a belated but finally compelling recognition of the gravity of these problems by officials and experts who had long resisted the obvious evidence of them. And with that recognition (as subsequent chapters will show) came the introduction of practices and policies, on the part of private groups as well as governmental agencies, designed to remedy those problems—to prosecute more forcefully minor as well as major crimes, to devolve welfare to states and localities, to give local churches and organizations more active roles in inner cities, to speak of "family values," not sarcastically, as was once the case, but respectfully, and to try to address, in myriad ways, the "moral decay" that is so widely deplored.

These efforts have not only had the salutary effect of reducing the incidence of crime, welfare, out-of-wedlock births, and the like. They have also begun to bring about a change in the moral temper of the country. Almost every account of the latest favorable statistics cites this as an important contributing factor. The *National Journal*, for example, reporting on a government study showing a decrease in teenage pregnancy, concludes that the decline was occasioned by "shifts in social norms," even more than by actual policies.[43] Another study, in the *Journal of the American Medical Association*, finds that "significant family factors," such as parental disapproval (not only of sexual activity among their children but also of their use of contraceptives), is a stronger deterrent to teenage pregnancy than contraception itself.[44] The Guttmacher Institute, reporting on the drop in the teenage birth rate, attributes it not only to the fear of AIDS and

better contraception, but also to "greater emphasis on abstinence . . . [and] more conservative attitudes about sex."[45]

Yet while there is much to be grateful for, there is little cause for
complacency. If the *rate* of births to teenagers and unmarried
women has decreased, partly because of a decline in the birthrate in general, the *ratio* of out-of-wedlock births (relative to all
births) has only leveled off, and at a very high level: one-third
of all children, two-thirds of black children, and three-fourths
of the children of teenagers are born out-of-wedlock.[46]* (And
the number of single-parent households with children continues to increase, from 24 percent in 1990 to 27 percent in 1996.)[48]
If there are fewer abortions, it is partly because of newer forms
of contraception (such as Norplant and Depo Provera), but also
because unmarried motherhood is more respectable. (And the
rate of abortions is still higher than in any other Western country.)[49] If older girls are less sexually active, younger ones (below
the age of fifteen) are more so.[50] (A new term, "tweens," has
been coined to describe eight-to-twelve-year-olds, who behave
more like teenagers than the "preadolescents" of old.)[51]

If divorce is declining, it is partly because cohabitation is
becoming more common; people living together without benefit of marriage can separate without benefit of divorce—and do
so with greater facility and frequency. Cohabitation increased by

---

*Those who would minimize the problem of out-of-wedlock births
cite birth rates rather than ratios.[47] But it is the proportion, not the
raw number, that is the more significant measure of social change,
because it determines the environment in which the next generation
of children is brought up. Among blacks, for example, the birth rate
for unmarried women has significantly declined, but since the rate for
married women has declined even further, the percentage of black
babies born out-of-wedlock has increased.

85 percent in the last decade alone, and eightfold since 1970; 40 percent of cohabiting couples separate before marriage; those who eventually marry have a 50 percent higher divorce rate than couples who did not live together before marriage; and the proportion of cohabiting mothers who eventually marry the child's father has declined by almost one-fourth in the last decade.[52]

If drug use among adults has fallen, that among young, and increasingly younger, people has risen. (In 1990, 27 percent of high-school seniors reported using marijuana in the previous year; in 1997, 38.5 percent did. For college seniors in the same period the rate rose from 29.4 percent to 31.6 percent).[53] If the fear of AIDS is one of the factors responsible for the decline in the out-of-wedlock birthrate among black women, it has not affected black men, among whom AIDS is significantly, and disproportionately, increasing. (While the death rate from HIV infection for white males fell from 15 per 100,000 in 1990 to 12.5 in 1996, that for black males rose from 44.2 to 66.4.)[54]

Even the notable decrease in crime, encouraging as it is, has some disconcerting aspects, criminologists warn us, for it reflects not only more effective policing and incarceration policies but also a decline in the number of teenagers. While the juvenile crime rate has fallen since 1993, juveniles are still responsible for a substantial portion of crime, and especially violent crime. (The FBI reports that while firearm killings by people above the age of twenty-five fell 44 percent between 1980 and 1997, such killings by eighteen- to twenty-four-year-olds rose by 20 percent.)[55] Some criminologists fear that the expected rise in the "baby-boomerang" cohort (the offsprings of baby-boomers) might lead to another "youth crime wave" comparable to that of the early 1990s.[56]

Moreover, the lowering or stabilization of some of the indices of social disarray does not begin to bring us back to the status quo ante, before their precipitous rise in the 1960s and '70s. One does not have to be nostalgic for a golden age that never was to appreciate the contrast between past and present.

The ratio of out-of-wedlock births has increased sixfold since 1960 (even the rate of out-of-wedlock births is one-third higher than it was in 1980); the number of children living with one parent has risen from less than one-tenth to more than one-quarter; and the number of households consisting of unmarried couples with children under the age of fifteen has grown from less than 200,000 in 1960 to over 1,300,000 in 1995.[57] It has often been observed that when Senator Daniel Patrick Moynihan wrote his percipient report on the breakdown of the black family in 1965, the black illegitimacy ratio was only slightly higher than the white ratio is today, and considerably lower than it is now for the country at large.[58] The divorce rate is almost twice that of the 1950s, and half of the marriages today and well over half of the remarriages are expected to end in divorce.[59] Sexual activity by teenage girls declined to 50 percent in 1995; but it had been less than 30 percent in 1970.[60] The serious crime rate is still considerably higher than in the fifties; homicides, which have witnessed the most dramatic decline, are 50 percent higher than they were in 1950; and homicides by fourteen- to seventeen-year-olds, half of what they were in 1993, are still double what they were in 1984.[61]

The statistics, moreover, good and bad, do not tell the whole story. The loss of parental authority, the lack of discipline in schools (to say nothing of knifings and shootings), the escalating violence and vulgarity on TV, the ready accessibility of pornography and sexual perversions on the Internet, the obscenity and sadism of videos and rap music, the binge-drinking and "hooking up" on college campuses, the "dumbing down" of education at all levels—these too are part of the social pathology of our time. And this pathology, which affects not only the "underclass" but the entire population, shows no signs of abating. "The morality of the cool," the cultural historian Roger Shattuck dubs a pervasive tendency in the culture, ranging from films that portray sadistic episodes in gory detail as if they were "cool," to the university, where sin and evil appear, in fashionable academic discourse, under the neutral or even positive guise of "transgression."[62]

Affluence and education, we have discovered, provide no immunity from moral and cultural disorders. Indeed, it has been argued that the affluent and well-educated bear some responsibility for the condition of the underclass. This is the thesis of a powerful book by Myron Magnet analyzing the symbiotic relationship between the "Haves" and the "Have-Nots."[63] It was the Haves, the cultural elites in the 1960s, who legitimized and glamorized the counterculture, which dislocated their own lives only temporarily but had a disastrous effect on those less fortunate than themselves. In disparaging the Puritan ethic, the counterculture undermined those virtues that might better have served the poor. The underclass is thus not only the victim of its own "culture of poverty"; it is also the victim of the upper-class culture around it. The kind of casual delinquency that a white suburban teenager can absorb with relative impunity may be literally fatal to a black inner city teenager. Or the child of an unmarried, affluent, professional woman (a "Murphy Brown") is obviously in a more privileged position than the child (more often, children) of an unmarried woman on welfare.

The effects of the culture, however, are felt at all levels. It was only a matter of time before there emerged, as Charles Murray has demonstrated, a white underclass with much the same pathology as the black.[64] And that pathology has affected the middle class as well. Some of the most affluent suburbs exhibit the same symptoms of teenage alcoholism, drug addiction, delinquency, and promiscuity, although not, obviously, to the same extent or with the same devastating results.

This situation is all the more distressing because it violates one of our most cherished assumptions: that moral progress is a necessary by-product of material progress. In fact, there has been much moral as well as material progress in recent decades—progress which is real and substantial even if it cannot always be measured statistically. As the result of a heightened social consciousness, abetted by judicious social legislation, we have witnessed the opening up of society to women, blacks, and other minorities; an increase of racial, religious, and sexual tolerance; a greater sensitivity to infirmities and inequities; an expansion of higher education, economic opportunity, and social mobility; a wider distribution of goods and comforts; an intellectual energy that has ushered in an era of unprecedented scientific, technological, and medical advances.

It does not belittle these considerable gains to observe the serious losses we have experienced during the same period. Indeed, the gains make the losses even more dismaying—losses, like the gains, that defy quantification. How do we measure the decline of civility, the loss of respect for privacy, the "repeal of reticence" (in Rochelle Gurstein's memorable phrase)[65] exhibited in all spheres of life—most conspicuously in television talk shows where participants proudly flaunt the most sordid details of their lives, but more insidiously, because seemingly high-minded, in the flood of confessional memoirs by writers exposing their own (or, worse, their spouse's, or lover's, or parent's) flaws and disabilities?* And how do we assess the relative weight of these gains and losses—the accession of freedom, candor, spontaneity, as against the decline of reserve, sensitivity, decency?

---

*A much praised memoir by the noted literary critic and novelist John Bayley recounted, while she was still alive, the most distressing details of the condition of his wife, the novelist and philosopher Iris Murdoch, who was suffering from Alzheimer's disease. That the memoir is written with consummate literary grace makes the betrayal of privacy even more shocking—all the more so because, as he makes clear, she herself always cherished that privacy.[66]

Senator Moynihan has encapsulated the social and cultural situation of our time in the brilliant phrase "defining deviancy down."[67] What was once stigmatized as deviant behavior is now tolerated and even sanctioned; what was once regarded as abnormal has been normalized. Thus, mental patients are no longer institutionalized; they are treated (and appear in the statistics) not as mentally incapacitated but merely as "homeless." So, too, out-of-wedlock births, once seen as betokening the breakdown of the family, are now viewed more benignly; in official reports they often appear as an "alternative mode of parenting." Among teenagers, oral sex is not regarded as a "sexual relation."

Charles Krauthammer has proposed a complementary concept, "defining deviancy up."[68] As deviancy is normalized, so what was once normal becomes deviant. The kind of family that has been regarded for centuries as natural and moral—the "bourgeois" family, as it is invidiously called—is now seen as pathological, concealing behind the facade of respectability the new "original sin," child abuse. Thus, while crime is underreported because we have become desensitized to it, child abuse is overreported, including cases, often inspired by therapists, recalled long after the supposed events. Similarly, rape has been "defined up" to encompass "date rape," which the participants themselves at the time might not have perceived as rape. Or smoking has been elevated to the rank of vice and sin, while sexual promiscuity is tolerated as a matter of individual right and choice.

The combined effect of defining deviancy down and up has been to normalize and legitimize what was once regarded as abnormal and illegitimate, and, conversely, to denigrate and discredit what was once proper and respectable. This redefinition of deviancy—and of morality—gives us a measure of the moral revolution that came in the wake of the cultural revolution. For some time, the very idea of morality—even the word itself—was rendered suspect, redolent of puritanism, conformism, repression, small-mindedness, and narrow-mindedness—a desire to "turn the clock back" to the stifling fifties, to an even more retrograde Victorianism, or, worse yet, to puritanism. ("Neo-Puritanism" is the latest epithet in this rhetorical war.[69])

Yet even here we may be witnessing a significant change in the temper of the times. Just as some of the social indices have taken a turn for the better, so has the willingness to entertain ideas that, only a few years ago, were derided or dismissed out of hand. In some circles "morality" and "virtue" are still regarded as code words for reaction and repression. But in others, and among the public at large, they testify to something real and commendable. If some analysts interpret the persistent and pervasive sense of moral decline as an exercise in nostalgia, the perennial illusion of a golden age, others credit it as a realistic appraisal of the present as compared with the past—realistic because it welcomes the recent improvement in some of our moral statistics while recognizing that that improvement leaves us far short of where we were not so very long ago.*

In this moral climate, appreciative of the gains we have made but also of the losses we have experienced, we may be emboldened (paraphrasing the Founding Fathers) to seek democratic remedies for the diseases incident to democratic society.

---

*Even nostalgia varies in degree. 70 percent of the public in 1998, but only 46 percent in 1965, thought that "young people today do not have as strong a sense of right and wrong as they did fifty years ago"; 71 percent in 1998, but only 52 percent in 1965, believed that "people in general do not lead lives as honest and moral as they used to."[70]

CHAPTER II
CIVIL SOCIETY: "THE SEEDBEDS
OF VIRTUE"

The most serious attempt to find a remedy for our moral disorders is the call for a restoration of civil society—families, communities, churches, civic and cultural organizations. This has been greeted with near-universal acclaim.* "Civil society" has become the mantra of our time. Liberals and conservatives, libertarians and communitarians, Democrats and Republicans, political scientists and politicians, religious and secular thinkers, agree about little else but this: that civil society is the key to our redemption.

There is something suspect about a concept that appeals to so many people of such different persuasions. And the confusion is compounded by the frequent use of "community" as a synonym for "civil society." From being a subset of civil society, "communities" (in the plural) have been elevated into "community" (in the singular). Yet the two concepts, civil society and community, have had very different histories and, until recently,

---

*Only "near-universal" acclaim. In academia, it has generated a debate with those liberals who maintain that civil society is not needed as a corrective to either individualism or statism because liberalism itself provides that corrective.[1]

very different connotations. Civil society has the function of mediating between the individual and the state, restraining the excessive individualism of the one and the overweening designs of the other, socializing the individual by imbuing him with a sense of duties and responsibilities as well as rights and privileges. Community has had a more collectivist, organic, integral character, recalling a tribal or feudal society (or a mythicized tribal or feudal society), in which individuals are socialized by being fused together in a single entity, a "solidarity."

The modern idea of civil society corresponds to what the nineteenth-century German sociologist Ferdinand Tönnies identified as *Gesellschaft,* in contrast to *Gemeinschaft,* or community. Today that distinction is a historical memory, community having lost its essentially organic character, even for those who now call themselves "communitarians." (The Israeli *kibbutzim* in their prime and the American "communes" of the 1960s were the last attempts to revive that older, romantic sense of community.) In contemporary parlance, a much emasculated idea of community retains some of the evocative appeal of the old term with little of its substance. Sociologists now speak of "small groups"—self-help and support groups (Alcoholics Anonymous being the prototype), Bible study and prayer fellowships, youth and singles clubs—as providing something of the emotional sustenance of community in the older sense. But unlike the community of old, these are voluntary, transient, often therapeutic groups that individuals freely move into and out of as the occasion requires.[2]

If "community" harks back to premodern times (or much idealized versions of those times), "civil society" has a distinctively modern pedigree.* The annalist of civil society can cite

---

*Aristotle's *koinonia politike* is sometimes cited as the classical source of "civil society," perhaps because of the Latin translation, *societas civilis.* But *koinonia politike* presumes the definition of man as *zoon politikon,* political animal, which belies any distinction between civil society and the *polis* (or state, as that word is now rendered). Even the family, as

John Locke's *Second Treatise on Government* (1690), where "the chief end" of civil society appears at one point as "the preservation of property," and at another as the means for the attainment of "safety, ease, and plenty."[4] Or David Hume's "Of the Origin of Government" (1741), where liberty is said to be "the perfection of civil society, but still authority must be acknowledged essential to its very existence."[5] Or Jean-Jacques Rousseau's *Discourse on Inequality* (1755), which starts by accepting Locke's premise about property and civil society ("the first man who, having enclosed a piece of ground, to whom it occurred to say 'this is mine' and found people sufficiently simple to believe him, was the true founder of civil society"), and goes on to vilify the "imposter" who let loose all the "crimes, wars, murders, . . . miseries and horrors" perpetrated in the name of property.[6] Or Adam Ferguson's *An Essay on the History of Civil Society* (1767), where the only substantive reference to civil society (apart from the title) is the statement that "it is in conducting the affairs of civil society, that mankind find the exercise of their best talents, as well as the object of their best affections."[7] Or Edmund Burke's *Reflections on the Revolution in France* (1790), which rebukes the French revolutionaries for acting as if they had "never been moulded into civil society, and had every thing to begin anew."[8]

These, however, are the archaeological exhumations of the historian, and are notably casual, imprecise, and inconsistent. It is not until Hegel's *Philosophy of Right* (1821) that the concept receives its first clear exposition. Praising civil society ("*die bürgerliche Gesellschaft*") as the "achievement of the modern world," Hegel identifies it as the intermediate sphere between the family and the state, "the battlefield where everyone's individual pri-

---

Aristotle understood it, was firmly located within the *polis*, the *polis* being "by nature clearly prior to the family and to the individual, since the whole is of necessity prior to the part."[3]

vate interest meets everyone else's"—and, more memorably, as "the territory of mediation where there is free play for every idiosyncrasy, every talent, every accident of birth and fortune, and where waves of every passion gush forth, regulated only by reason glinting through them."[9]

It is not Hegel, however, who is generally associated with the concept, but Alexis de Tocqueville. The term appears several times in *Democracy in America* (1835 and 1840), but only in passing, and not at all in the very many chapter titles or in the index to the English editions. In the original translation of the book by Henry Reeve, one reference to "la société civile" was translated as "social intercourse."[10] This mistranslation persisted for well over a century throughout the many editions of the work in both England and the United States, including the two-volume Knopf edition in 1948 which was influential in reviving interest in Tocqueville in the United States.[11] Not until 1966, in a new translation edited by J. P. Mayer and Max Lerner, was this corrected.[12] And not until then (or after then) did "civil society" became identified with the "voluntary associations" that Tocqueville spoke of so frequently and admiringly.

In view of the current popularity of civil society, it is extraordinary how recently—within the last decade or two—not only the term but the idea came into general circulation. In retrospect, one might think that it was the encounter with Nazism and Communism that prompted its revival. If Hannah Arendt, in *The Origins of Totalitarianism* (1951), was right in saying (as she surely was) that the atomization and isolation of the individual was the distinctive strategy of totalitarianism, the enemies of totalitarianism might well have looked to civil society as the countervailing force, the "territory of mediation," as Hegel put it, designed to thwart that despotism. By the same token, the subversion and manipulation of the family by Nazism and Communism might have prompted us to include the family in

the realm of civil society (as Hegel did not) as the most important of those mediating institutions. Yet not until well after the
experience of totalitarianism did the idea of civil society
become popular in the United States and in most of the Western world. It does not appear in Arendt's book (which cites
Tocqueville, but only in reference to the *ancien régime* and the
correspondence with Arthur Gobineau on the subject of race).[13]*
Nor is it discussed in most works on totalitarianism. Nor, prior
to the 1980s, is it an entry in encyclopedias, dictionaries, indexes
to periodical literature, and other reference works.[15]

What has recently inspired, in the United States at least, a
spate of books, articles, conferences, colloquia, commissions,
and organizations promoting civil society is not a belated recognition of the horrors of totalitarianism but a response to the
moral and cultural disorders of democracy itself. And it is as a
remedy to these disorders that the idea of civil society is now
invoked.

It is an attractive idea because it calls upon nothing more
than such natural, familiar, universal institutions as families and
communities. Moreover, it is preeminently a democratic idea. It
is democracy on the smallest scale—the "little platoon" that
Burke described as "the first principle (the germ as it were) of
public affections."[16] It is also an attribute of democracy on the
largest scale—Tocqueville's "voluntary associations" which have
the crucial task of mediating between the individual and the
state. In addition, it serves as a corrective to that other democratic flaw identified by Tocqueville: "the tyranny of the major-

---

*Although Hannah Arendt does not use the term "civil society," some
of her later writings are severely critical of the concept. In *The Human
Condition* (1958), she objects to the modern idea of the "private,"
which she identifies with "social relations" or "society," as opposed to
the classical idea of the "public," the *polis*.[14] That "private" or "social"
realm is what today would be called "civil society."

ity," the power of the collective mass of the people which may be inimical to the liberty of individuals and minorities.

Today, civil society is asked to assume yet another task: that of repairing the moral fabric of democratic society. The institutions of civil society, we are told, are the "seedbeds of virtue."[17] It is here, in families and communities, that character takes shape, children become civilized and socialized, people acquire a sense of social as well as individual responsibility, rights are complemented by duties, self-interest is reconciled with the general interest, and civility mutes the discord of opposing wills. And all this is achieved naturally, organically, without the artificial contrivances of government, without the passage of laws or the intrusion of bureaucracies, without recourse to the coercive, punitive power of the state.

The principle is admirable. Today more than ever we have need of a mediating structure between an unrestrained individualism and an overly powerful state, between the "unencumbered self" (in Michael Sandel's memorable phrase)[18] and the "nanny state." Too many years of an intrusive government have left some of the most important institutions of civil society in an enervated and demoralized condition. The welfare state has usurped the traditional function of families in the care of the sick and the aged. Public schools have displaced parents in instructing the young in sex education. Private charities are often little more than conduits of the state for the distribution of public funds (and are obliged to distribute them in accord with the requirements of government bureaucracies). And the marketplace, which Hegel saw as one of the principal components of civil society, has been subjected on the one hand to the regulatory mechanisms of the state, and on the other to the economic process of "creative destruction" that subverts the traditional institutions and bourgeois ethos upon which capitalism once depended.

For a while there was a flurry of concern about what Robert Putnam called the "bowling alone" phenomenon: while Americans are bowling more than ever, they are doing so "solo" rather than in the leagues that were once so popular. Buttressed by statistics showing the decrease of membership in other voluntary associations, Putnam took this as a sign of America's "declining social capital," the "disappearance of civic America."[19] Those statistics, and the thesis in general, have since been disputed. If bowling leagues are no longer popular, they have been replaced by baseball leagues and a host of other organized activities, as well as a plethora of "small groups" devoted to one or another specific purpose.[20]

In fact, the problem today would seem to be not an insufficiency of civil society, but its deformation. Some institutions are flourishing as never before, indeed, are more powerful than ever before. Trade unions and trade associations, philanthropies and foundations, universities and cultural organizations, are often so large and influential that they are, in effect, quasi-governmental institutions. They do not so much mediate between the individual and the state as impose themselves upon the individual with the tacit collusion of the state. In some instances they carry more weight than public agencies. At crucial periods in the recent history of education, the Ford Foundation and the National Education Association, singly or together, have been more influential than local or state governments in shaping the character and quality of the public schools. These institutions are not quite what Tocqueville, or his disciples, had in mind by "voluntary associations." So far from being voluntary, some are very nearly mandatory; in many industries, it is obligatory for employees to join a union, as it is for employers to belong to a trade association.

Some theorists of civil society, wanting to rescue the concept from these large, bureaucratic, quasi-public institutions, would confine it to small, local, personal, face-to-face groups—not the National Education Association but local parent-teacher

associations, not the Ford Foundation but small family foundations, not the Red Cross but community soup kitchens. Other
theorists, impressed by the technological revolution that is altering all of society, would enlarge the concept by extending it to
the Internet and cyberspace, on the theory that this is where
many people today find their real (that is, "virtual") communities and associations.[21]

If the structure of civil society is in doubt, so is its function.
Civil society is meant to serve not only as a mediating force
between the individual and the state, but also as a moralizing
force for both the individual and society. But here too some
of the most prominent institutions of civil society have had
ambiguous effects. Private foundations and universities have
promoted educational ideologies (the "self-esteem" philosophy,
for example) that are antithetical to the kind of moral character
that civil society is meant to encourage. Local cable stations
bring soft-core and even hard-core pornography into the living
room. Museums and civic organizations all too often give their
imprimatur to meretricious and obscene exhibits that pass as
art. And the family, the most basic unit of civil society, is in an
especially fragile condition, hardly a model of stability and
responsibility.

Civil society has been described as an "immune system against
cultural disease."[22] But much of it has been infected by the same
virus that produced that disease—the ethical and cultural relativism that reduces all values, standards, and institutions to
expressions of personal will and power. If civil society is to
become an effective instrument of social mediation and reformation, it will have to reaffirm the moral principles that give it
its distinctive purpose. And it can do that only by exercising its
authority and using the social sanctions available to it, sanctions
that may be as coercive, psychologically if not physically, as the
legal sanctions imposed by the state. These mechanisms of

approbation and disapprobation are all the more necessary in a liberal society, for the more effective the social sanctions, the less need there is for the legal and penal sanctions of the state. Some of the advocates of civil society—the "hard" advocates—know this. They value civil society precisely because it is a warrant for a liberal society, a protection against the excesses of both individualism and statism. And because they are serious about limiting those excesses, they are prepared to endow civil society with the authority to do just that—to restore not only the institutions of civil society but the force of social and moral suasion.

The "soft" proponents of civil society pay lip service to the idea but lack the will or conviction to implement it. They are pleased to acclaim charity and compassion as virtues, but not to stigmatize egotism and hedonism as vices. Indeed, they are uncomfortable with the words "vice" and "stigmatize," as if it is not precisely the function of civil society to encourage virtue and discourage—that is, stigmatize—vice. Don Eberly, one of the most thoughtful proponents of civil society, describes this wing of the movement as "civic revivalists," seeking the greater participation of people in local communities and associations but only for the purpose of "civic revival" rather than "moral revival." "What we don't need," he quotes the political scientist Benjamin Barber, "is moral character, but civic character. Our aim is democratic citizens; not the moral man. A society does not need moral truths; we need to live together."[23]

Others, although not dismissive of morality in principle, are wary of its implementation. They deplore the excessive autonomy of the individual and the proliferation of rights, but are not prepared to take the practical measures that would effectively limit that autonomy and those rights. They may even use civil society as a means of evading the hard choices involved in any social policy. Thus, an influential communitarian proposes to restore the family "without reviving a 1950s mentality"; to stop criminals and drunk drivers "without opening the door—even a crack—to a police state"; to curb the spread of AIDS "while protecting privacy"; to discourage divorce without restricting it in any way[24]—as if criminality, drunken driving, AIDs, or divorce can be curbed without restrictions on privacy and individuality.

Two recent studies of actual communities (rather than theoretical disquisitions on the idea of community)—Alan Ehrenhalt's *The Lost City* on Chicago in the 1950s,[25] and David Gelernter's *1939* on the New York World's Fair [26]—make it clear that moral authority is an essential attribute of healthy, vigorous communities. Neither writer is unduly sentimental or celebratory about those now historic times. They are fully aware of the extent of crime and corruption (in Chicago more than New York) and the disabilities under which women and, far more seriously, blacks lived and labored. But they are also appreciative of the vitality of those communities, of what made them genuine communities. What Ehrenhalt says of Chicago after the war might have been echoed by Gelernter about New York on the eve of the war: "The Chicago of the 1950s was a time and place in which ordinary people lived with good and evil, right and wrong, sins and sinners, in a way that is almost incomprehensible to most of us on the other side of the 1960s moral deluge."[27] That sense of stability and moral consensus has been irrevocably lost, Ehrenhalt claims, because we have reneged on the "bargain" we then made: the purchase of stability and morality at the cost of restrictions on liberty.[28] In a more recent essay, he makes the point even more sharply. "Authority and community," he says, "have in fact unraveled together," but whereas people are nostalgic for the loss of community, "authority possesses very few mourners."[29]

If some proponents of civil society emasculate it by depriving it of its social authority, others do so by making it, in effect, an adjunct of the welfare state. Where the hard advocates of civil society seek to strengthen civil society by transferring to the family, church, community, and voluntary associations many of the functions currently exercised by the state, the soft advocates either ignore the subject of the welfare state as if it has no bearing on civil society, or take issue with some aspects of it while endorsing it in general. Some go so far as to argue that the civic or communitarian impulse that sustains civil society is also the justification for the welfare state, which is simply the community writ large. Michael Sandel rejects the ideas of individual rights and redistributive justice that traditional liberals invoke to justify the welfare state, but defends the welfare state itself as a means of "affirming the membership and forming the civic identity of rich and poor alike."[30]

This partiality for the welfare state may account for the fact that many communitarians are more solicitous of community in the abstract than of particular communities that may challenge the primacy of the welfare state by taking over some of its functions. It is revealing that the singular "community" appears more often in the literature of communitarianism than the plural "communities."* Michael Walzer goes so far as to speak of families, neighborhoods, and clubs as merely "analogues" of the larger political community, which he identifies not only with the welfare state but with "social democracy"[31]—"socialism with a human face," one might say.

Communitarianism in this sense may also be said to be Clintonism with a human face. In his State of the Union Message in 1996, the President used the word "community" fifteen times. His conception of community, however, is so expansive as to embrace the entire country—"the American community," as he

---

*It is also ironic that this singular idea of "community" persists in spite of the fragmentization that has taken place in recent years as a result of multiculturalism, affirmative action, radical feminism, and the conflicting imperatives of the race/class/gender schema. There is, in fact, little coherence or commonality left in the "community" that is at the heart of communitarianism.

says.[32] One is reminded of Governor Mario Cuomo's address to the Democratic Convention in 1988 when he extolled the idea of "family"—America as one large, happy family.

At the opposite pole of the communitarian view of civil society is the libertarian one. Rigorous libertarians, to be sure, are hostile to the very idea of civil society on the grounds that society, as much as the state, is an illegitimate limitation on the individual. In their defense, they may cite John Stuart Mill's *On Liberty*, which argued that the peculiarly modern threat to liberty is not governmental despotism but "social tyranny." In response to this new form of tyranny Mill formulated his "one very simple principle": that liberty could be restricted only for the purpose of self-protection or the prevention of harm to others. Apart from this one condition, neither "physical force in the form of legal penalties" nor "the moral coercion of public opinion" could be permitted to interfere with the liberty of the individual.[33]

Moderate libertarians take a more benign view of civil society.[34] Indeed, they rely upon it as the only effective antidote to the state, the sole force capable of exercising the social functions that have been usurped by the state. It is in civil society, they reason, that individuals can freely join together for common purposes without the intrusion of government; it is there that they can choose to be moral, to develop a sense of social responsibility and discharge their social duties. But this can happen only if the state is entirely excluded from civil society. So long as the state is even partially involved, it is bound to undermine the authority of civil society and thus inhibit the moral maturation as well as the liberty of the individual.

This is a powerful rebuttal to those soft proponents of civil society who try to reconcile it with the welfare state. But even this modified libertarian version may not fully take into account the degree of moral and social coercion, and thus the limitation on liberty and individuality, implicit in civil society as a whole or in the particular institutions of civil society—institutions that truly serve as the "seedbeds of virtue."

The dilemmas of civil society have emerged most dramatically in Central and Eastern Europe. Unlike the United States and Western Europe, the concept arose there in response to totalitarianism—not to Nazism, but to the prolonged domination of the Soviet Union. The rise of the Solidarity movement in Poland in the late 1970s and '80s inspired a call for "the rebirth of civil society." (Leszek Kolakowski, Poland's most distinguished émigré, referred to this as a "post-revolutionary hangover."[35]) Instead of trying to reform the political structure of the Communist state, the dissidents sought to bypass the state by building a democratic, pluralistic order in civil society—a "parallel society," as they put it.[36]* Meeting surreptitiously in churches and the back rooms of bars, circulating the *samizdats* that kept alive the spirit of freedom, creating "flying universities" to rival the official ones, the dissidents not only fostered the idea of civil society but in those very activities created something very like a civil society, a refuge from the oppressive Communist regime.

Yet the society that arose after the downfall of Communism fell far short of the ideal. Instead of being independent of the state, the idea of civil society served to legitimize the new government, as if the purposes of civil society were fulfilled in the elected parliaments and administrative agencies of the state.[38] "The myth of civil society," reports the Polish intellectual Alek-

---

*Some theorists derive this strategy from Antonio Gramsci, who claimed that this is the way the bourgeoisie exercises its rule, not through the coercion of the state but through the "hegemony" of society. But Gramsci's "civil society" included political parties as well as family, community, and voluntary associations, and was sometimes almost indistinguishable from the state.[37]

sander Smolar, was "one of the first casualties of the postcommunist era. . . . What had been 'moral civil societies' became political blocs—first in opposition, and then, with the decomposition of the old ruling structures, in power." Those dissidents who had extolled the idea of civil society now put forward the idea of a "normal society"—normality meaning a political state complete with constitutional democracy and the rule of law. This ideological shift was accompanied by the actual transfer of prominent activists from the institutions of civil society— human rights groups, publishing enterprises, educational centers—into the agencies of government. As an "especially poignant example," Smolar cites the mass recruitment of young people from the pacifist group Freedom and Peace into the new Ministry of Home Affairs, which includes the political police.[39]

"Normal society," it soon became apparent (not only in Poland but throughout East Europe), was a far cry from the "moral civil society" that had been envisaged. Indeed, the new societies often conspicuously lacked those virtues that had been thought to be inherent in the very idea of civil society. In 1992, Václav Havel, then president of Czechoslovakia, reflected on the unanticipated consequences of a liberation that threatened to liberate his countrymen not only from the tyranny of Communism but from the constraints of morality.

> The return of freedom to a place that became morally unhinged has produced something that it clearly had to produce, and therefore something we might have expected. But it has turned out to be far more serious than anyone could have predicted: an enormous and blindingly visible explosion of every imaginable human vice. A wide range of questionable or at least ambivalent human tendencies . . . has suddenly been liberated, as it were, from its straitjacket and given free rein at last. . . . Thus we are witnesses to a bizarre state of affairs: society has freed itself, true, but in some ways it behaves worse than when it was in chains.[40]

Those who are dismayed by the anarchic character of civil society in parts of Eastern Europe and Russia often attribute this to capitalist "greed." What they have yet to discover—indeed, what Communism should have taught them—is that public institutions can be as self-serving as private ones, that power and ideology can be as corrupting as money, that Communist vices have been no less vicious (and far more deadly) than capitalist ones, and Communist culture no less degrading.

This experience may turn out to be a defining moment for the democratic West as well as for post-Communist Europe. The idea of civil society in its Tocquevillian sense, as a mediating force between an excessive individualism and an oppressive state, is as valid and crucial for the old democracies as for the new. But for the old democracies as for the new, it is not enough, as Havel discovered, to restore civil society; it is also necessary to reform and remoralize its institutions. It is this process of reformation and remoralization that now engages the hard advocates of civil society as they confront the hard problems of democratic society—education, welfare, crime, popular culture, and above all, the family.

CHAPTER III

THE FAMILY: "A MINIATURE
SOCIAL SYSTEM"

If civil society itself is problematic, the family, the bedrock of society—civil society writ small, as it were—is no less so. This is all the more troubling because the family, even more than civil society, is the "seedbed of virtue," the place where we receive our formative experiences, where the most elemental, primitive emotions come into play and we learn to express and control them, where we come to trust and relate to others, where we acquire habits of feeling, thinking, and behaving that we call character—where we are, in short, civilized, socialized, and moralized. The family, it is said, is a "miniature social system, with parents as the chief promotors and enforcers of social order."[1] Today, unfortunately, many parents are as ineffectual in promoting and enforcing social order as are other authorities, and that miniature system is as weak and unreliable as the larger social system of which it is part.

When Joseph Schumpeter warned his readers of the self-destructive effect of capitalism, its tendency to subvert the bourgeois ethos upon which its economic success depends, he also warned of the "disintegration of the bourgeois family." Writing in 1942, long before the rates of divorce, out-of-wedlock births, and single-parenthood had started their steep ascent, he pointed out that statistics did not tell the whole story. "It does not matter how many marriages are dissolved by judicial decree—what matters is how many lack the content essential to the old pattern." The disintegration of the family, he argued, is caused by the inveterate habit of rationalization that characterizes capitalism and that has been extended to private life. By "a sort of inarticulate system of cost accounting," people have come to believe that the advantages of a family fail to compensate for the disadvantages—not only the economic costs of maintaining the family but "the loss of comfort, of freedom from care, and opportunity to enjoy alternatives of increasing attractiveness and variety." What is forgotten is the great contribution of parenthood to physical and moral health—"to 'normality' as we might express it." Focused on the immediate and the visible, we tend to be impatient with the demands of family life because we ignore the "hidden necessities of human nature or of the social organism." It was not always so, Schumpeter reminds us. For *homo oeconomicus*, the original bourgeois man, the family was the mainspring of the profit motive. He was moved "to work and to save primarily for wife and *children*" (Schumpeter's italics)—for the future of his family rather than his present wants or needs. Modern man, by contrast, tends to have a "time-horizon" limited to his own life expectancy, as a result of which he loses the incentive not only to work, save, and invest but also to raise and nurture a family.[2]

Schumpeter's may be an overly utilitarian and rationalistic explanation.* But he was brilliantly prescient in his analysis of a culture that, although not consciously hostile to the family, is

---

*But perhaps not. A professor of sociology at Bologna University, commenting on the recent decline of the size of the family in Italy, unwittingly echoes Schumpeter: "Prosperity has strangled us. Comfort is now the only thing anybody believes in. The ethic of sacrifice for a family—one of the basic ideas of human societies—has become a historical notion."[3]

less than hospitable to it, a culture too present-minded and self-centered to tolerate the kinds of constraints imposed on parents in the interests of the family—or for that matter, the constraints on children, who are no less present-minded and self-centered. Nineteenth- and early-twentieth-century accounts of working-class life are replete with stories of children laboring part-time and contributing their meager earnings not only willingly but proudly to the family. Today children commonly receive allowances from their parents to be spent for their personal satisfaction.

The family now seems to be in a more perilous state than capitalism, for the reasons Schumpeter foresaw, and many others. If he had few statistics to support his intuitions, we have all too many—statistics of divorce, single-parenthood, out-of-wedlock births, cohabitation.* We also have another set of statistics correlating the breakdown of the family with the indices of social pathology. Single-mother households, for example, have more than triple the poverty rate of married-couple households and are eight times as likely to remain in poverty for two years or longer.[6] Or young men who have grown up in homes without fathers are twice as probable (and those with stepfathers three times as probable) to end up in jail as those who come from two-parent families (keeping constant such other factors as race, income, parent's education, and urban residence).[7] Or (refuting the familiar racial stereotype) the school drop-out rate for white

---

*It has been said that a longer historical perspective shows the crisis of the family going back a century or more; the divorce rate increased as much as fifteenfold between 1870 and 1920, so that by 1924 one in seven marriages ended in dissolution.[4] These figures, however, are misleading, for the fifteenfold increase was from a very low base. And a divorce rate of one in seven is qualitatively different from the present one in two.[5]

children living with a single parent is substantially higher (28 percent) than that of black children living with two parents (17 percent).[8] It is findings such as these that make other statistics so ominous—most notably, the fact that more than one-quarter of children (and twice that proportion of black children) live in single-parent homes, a threefold rise since 1960.[9]

~ Yet even now there is a reluctance to face up to the true nature of the problem. The battered-woman syndrome has been much publicized, but some of the essential facts have been obscured by the "nonjudgmental" rhetoric that often accompanies these accounts—the failure, for example, to distinguish between marriage and cohabitation. David Blankenhorn, the director of the Institute for American Values, points out that domestic violence is habitually referred to as "marital violence" or "wife-beating," while the perpetrators are called "husbands" or "partners" (or lumped together in the single category of "husbands and partners") regardless of their legal status. ("Intimates" is another common euphemism.) Thus it is husbands who are generally represented as the guilty parties and marriage is made to appear as the locus of the problem, although it is the nonmarital relationship that is far more often associated with violence.[10] A Department of Justice study finds that a woman is three times more likely to be raped or sexually assaulted by a boyfriend and ten times by an acquaintance than by a spouse.[11]

It is also well known that children are more likely to be abused in broken families than in intact ones, by stepfathers more often than biological fathers, and still more often by mothers' boyfriends.[12] And, not infrequently, by mothers in such households, under the pressure of drugs, alcohol, or abusive men. The Family Preservation Act of 1992 was passed on the assumption that the biological mother is the natural guardian of her children. This act was amended five years later, after a series of well-publicized, horrific cases of child deaths in which the mother was responsible or complicitous. Under the amended act, the safety of the child is regarded as paramount, rather than the "right" of the mother or the "unity" of the family, so that an abused child can be removed from a household headed by a biological but acutely "dysfunctional" parent. There is also a growing sentiment for the placing of such children in orphanages (or "public boarding schools," as they are euphemistically called) rather than foster homes, which too often reproduce the unfortunate conditions of the original home.[13]

The effects of divorce and single-parenthood on children are more subtle and far-reaching than physical abuse. Longitudinal surveys find that the children of single-parent affluent blacks do more poorly in college than the children of intact black families with lower incomes; the daughters of white single parents are five times more likely to have children out of wedlock than the daughters of married parents; and on all indices of well-being, children with stepparents do about the same as those with single parents and significantly less well than those living with both biological parents. One study concludes that "children who grow up in a household with only one biological parent are worse off, on average, than children who grow up in a household with both of their biological parents," this regardless of race, educational background, or remarriage.[14]

Other studies suggest that even the long-term health of children is affected by the breakup of the family. The average lifespan of children whose parents were divorced while the children were below the age of twenty-one is significantly lower than that of children whose parents had not been divorced. Moreover, the children of divorced parents are themselves more likely to be divorced, and since divorced adults tend to die earlier, such children are at double jeopardy of premature death.[15] The old adage that parents should stay together for the sake of the children may be truer than was once thought.

That adage may now have to be amended to read that parents should also stay together for their own sakes. The death rates for currently married men and women are half of the rates for those of similar age who have been divorced, and less than half for those who have never married. (On the other hand, the mortality rate of widows is almost that of women who have never married, and that of widowers is significantly higher than that of bachelors—perhaps because the happily married mourn their dead spouses?)[16] It is marriage, moreover, not cohabitation, that correlates with health. Cohabiting women are more than twice as likely to be the victims of domestic violence than married women; they have three times the rate of depression; and couples who cohabited before marriage report significantly lower levels of marital happiness and sexual satisfaction than other couples. (They also have higher rates of divorce.)[17]

As these statistics have become more conclusive, those who support "diverse" and "alternative" forms of family life have shifted the grounds of their defense, disputing not the statistics themselves but the very use of statistics.* Judith Stacey, a prominent member of this school, protests against any social science research that suggests the superiority of "the 1950s family." "The best antidote to this sort of thing," she says, "is not necessarily more social science but an immersion in the lived values of actual families"—narratives of nontraditional families that defy the statistics. The psychiatrist Robert Coles is similarly suspicious of social science as a barometer of the family. "Storytelling," he says, rather than statistics, "allows for a spaciousness about our day-to-day existence"; and fictional stories, mixing "literal truth and imaginative renderings," are as compelling as real ones.[18]

---

*A similar shift took place in the controversy over the standard of living of English workers as a result of the industrial revolution. When the quantitative evidence made it clear that the standard had actually risen, radical historians moved the debate to the "quality of life" of the workers, which could not be measured quantitatively.

. . .

But stories, true stories, reveal much the same facts as the statistics. And history bears out much of Schumpeter's theory. Historically, the family, whether the nuclear family of "bourgeois man" or the extended family of his ancestors, has been the most enduring of social relationships. (In fact, the nuclear family is much older than is commonly thought.) Unlike the other institutions of civil society, the family has never been seen as a "voluntary association." It has been a "given" of life, an immutable fact, starting before birth (in the lives of parents and grandparents) and persisting after death (in the lives of children and grandchildren). Because the family has had this involuntary, mandatory character, it has also been assumed to have the authority to carry out its primary functions: the rearing and socializing of children and the caring for its weakest and most vulnerable members, the old and the young. At its best, it was the source of unconditional love as well as of unconditional responsibility. At its worst, if it failed in its prescriptive mission, it was subject to social as well as legal sanctions.

At least so it once was. Today the family has been "voluntarized," as it were; it is whatever we choose to make of it. The English sociologist Jeffrey Weeks commends the new family as the "family of choice." "For many people today family means something more than biological affinity. It means something you create for yourself, something that involves interactions, commitment and obligations that have to be negotiated in a world where nothing is pre-given or certain. In such families, he explains, friends are as important as relatives. Thus we move in and out of families at will. This is the meaning of divorce, serial marriages, cohabitation, single-parentage, and "alternative lifestyles." The "family of choice" is defined not by ties of blood, marriage, or adoption, but by varieties of relationships and habitations among "autonomous," "consensual" adults and their offspring.

It is not only academics who have thus reconfigured the family. The Episcopal Church, one commentator is pleased to report, has escaped the "trap of nostalgia." Instead of regarding the family in its antiquated, narrow, legal sense, the church now recognizes that it is a social institution embracing "a broad range of kin and nonkin relationships in a variety of racial and economic settings." In this "emerging theology of family," the report goes on, "'household' replaces an outmoded, stereotyped 'family.'"[20]

The effect of this liberalization and voluntarization of the family is to release it (or its postmodern version) from its traditional obligations. We speak of the dysfunctional family as one of the characteristics of the underclass. But a great many middle-class families have also become, to one degree or another, dysfunctional, as the newly liberated family ceases to be a stable, reliable force either for its members or for society. The "1950s family," as is now said pejoratively—one that was presumed to have two married, resident, responsible parents—did not always correspond to that ideal. There were notable exceptions and deviations: divorced parents, widowed mothers, drunken fathers, abused wives, mistreated and delinquent children. But they were understood to be just that, exceptions and deviations, misfortunes of circumstance or failings of character. A very large majority of families did in fact conform to the two-parent model, and couples did not marry with the expectation that half of them would, sooner or later, be divorced. If the Norman Rockwell image of the 1950s family, complete with two happy, tow-haired children (always one girl and one boy), was idealized and romanticized, the current caricature of it as a bourgeois, patriarchal, authoritarian institution designed to oppress the wife, abuse the children, and inhibit sexuality is no less remote from the reality.

It is not only the social ethos that has changed the status of the family; it is the intrusion of the state. Two centuries ago, Adam

Smith could confidently declare: "The father is obliged to bring up his children, and the children in case of old age or infirmity to maintain the father."[21] The modern state has helped put an end to that. By subsidizing poor fatherless families it sends the message that the father is dispensable because the state can be counted on to assume the traditional paternal functions. And by — subsidizing aged or infirm parents (non-poor as well as poor), it relieves children of their normal filial functions. Only a few generations ago, it was regarded as shameful for an old person to be dependent upon public relief—shameful for the parent and for the child. Today a parent regards it as shameful to be "beholden" to a child, and the child (even a child of means) feels absolved of any moral, let alone legal, responsibility for a parent, believing that responsibility to lie with the state. Cases of severe need which were beyond the resources of the family were formerly assisted by public relief, private charity, or self-insuring "friendly societies." With the very best intentions, we undertook to regularize, legalize, and expand that assistance. Relief, renamed welfare, became a legal right, an entitlement from the state. The unwitting effect of this policy was to undermine the traditional family by depriving parents and children of their customary obligations and expectations.*

*And not only the unwitting effect. The social-engineering impulse on the part of planners and reformers has always made them suspicious of the family, and this long before the welfare state. Christopher Lasch points out that the Progressive movement at the turn of the century tried to establish, as the principal socializing agent for the child, the supposedly enlightened, rational, efficient public school system, in place of the erratic family that veered between being overly tyrannical and overly indulgent. Whereas the mother, Progressives argued, cared only for "my child," the school had a larger, impersonal, objective view of "the child."[22] One might add that, for somewhat different reasons, Marxists and utopian socialists, long before the Progressive era, displayed the same distrust of the family. (And before them, of course, Plato.)

The state has also undermined the family by policies that belittle the importance of marriage and even make it disadvantageous to be married, thus "de-privileging," in the current jargon, marriage itself. In public housing and social work agencies, the distinction between the unmarried and married is being eliminated on the grounds that such a distinction is discriminatory. Where poor married couples once received preferential treatment, today the unmarried, because they are apt to be poorer, obtain more of the benefits of the state—a bonus, in effect, for being unmarried. The intentions behind these reforms may be admirable, but the consequence is to weaken an already enervated family structure.

If the state has usurped some of the functions of the family, the sexual revolution has subverted the very conception of the traditional family. Conservatives as well as liberals may be dismayed by the attention paid in recent years to so private and personal a matter as sexual morality. But the reason this has loomed so large is because sexual morality is never a purely private or personal affair. It is at the heart of the idea and the institution of the family. If the family is the primal agent of socialization, the place where we develop those habits of love, trust, and responsibility that make us mature human beings, adultery is a violation of the family, a betrayal of love, trust, and responsibility, an act of infidelity and irresponsibility. When Hillary Clinton rebuked those who were making an issue of her husband's affair with Monica Lewinsky, she invoked the claim of privacy. "The only people," she said, "who count in any marriage are the two that are in it"[23]—forgetting the children who are surely a party to marriage, to say nothing of the integrity and dignity of the family itself.

The sexual revolution has brought about a double liberation: a liberation *within* marriage, altering the relations and roles of men, women, and children within the family; and also a liberation *from* marriage, making it easier to leave or dispense with the family—to have extramarital affairs and nonmarital "relationships." It has also had the paradoxical effect of undermining social policies that liberals as well as conservatives generally favor. Local and state governments, for example, may try to enforce the obligation of a father to support his children, but this policy is subverted by a welfare system that provides an alternative means of support, as well as by a culture that derides the idea of the father as the natural "head" of the family—that even denies the idea of the father as a necessary member of the family. Feminists would surely object to Adam Smith's dictum that the father is obliged to bring up his children; they would amend it so that a "parent" has that obligation. Their intention is to elevate the mother, raise her to a status of equality with the father. But the effect may be to burden her with an economic and psychological responsibility she cannot bear.

This burden is all the more onerous today because so many more mothers are working outside the home. In 1960, a little over 30 percent did so; today twice that number do.[24] Here too we find the ambiguous effects of good intentions. The opportunity to have a career, to be liberated from the confines of family and domesticity (and also from economic and psychological dependency upon husbands), has been the goal of feminists for well over a century. But having realized that goal, many women are discovering that it has been purchased at considerable cost. A career, they find, is even more demanding for the woman than for the man, because she still has (whatever some feminists might insist and some obliging husbands might concede) the primary responsibility for the care of the children. Many women are also becoming disillusioned with the commonly proposed solution to this problem, government-subsidized day care. Even the best day care, they are finding (and most of it is far from the best), is inferior to ordinary parental care in the home. Thus many mothers are seeking ways to accommodate family and work, often by abandoning the conventional employment or career pattern. Single mothers who work out of economic necessity have no or few alternatives, but married women who work to supplement the family income may decide to forgo the amenities provided by that additional income, at least in the early years of their children. Or they may choose to work part-time, or at home, or with flexible work schedules. The pursuit of a career, more and more women are coming to realize (as men are as well), is not an absolute good, either for themselves or for their families.

Most recently we have been confronted with yet another challenge to the family. In addition to the sexual, social, and ideological revolutions, we now have a demographic revolution to contend with—a population "implosion" quite as momentous as the population "explosion" predicted for so long. The latest statistics suggest a decline of the birth rate in Western countries that will have unprecedented results. Economists worry about a "graying" population with fewer young people to sustain the large number of elderly, putting a great strain upon social security, pensions, health care, and government finances in general. But the consequences for the family are no less momentous. The demographer Nicholas Eberstadt calculates that if Italy's present fertility rate of 1.2 continues for only two generations, almost three-fifths of that nation's children will have "no siblings, cousins, aunts, or uncles; they will have only parents, grandparents, and perhaps great-grandparents." In other Western countries, with a somewhat higher birth rate (the European average is 1.4 and the American about 2.0), the effect would be only slightly different: two-fifths would have no collateral relatives.[25] Thus we now have to worry not only about children without fathers but about children without kinfolk—children brought up in families so attenuated as hardly to warrant the name "family" at all.

. . .

The family, like civil society, is obviously in need of revitalization and reformation, of recovering the legal and social authority it has forfeited to the state and the moral authority it has ceded to the counterculture. The precondition for such a revitalization and reformation has already been met in the increasing attention paid to the subject and the exemplary body of research that has accumulated. The family (again like civil society) has spawned a host of societies, conferences, commissions, journals, and books in the past decade or two, producing a good deal of hard-headed analysis of the actual state of affairs and an equally hard-headed willingness to entertain reforms that may go against the grain of current dispositions and practices.*

This is not to say that we are obliged to return to the model family (or mythicized model) of the 1950s, with its prescribed parental roles and relations. If, as the burden of scholarship now suggests, the two-parent family is generally (although not in every instance) most conducive to the welfare of children as well as society, there is much room within that family structure for improvement—for greater security, stability, and flexibility. And much can be done outside it to promote the same values, to encourage marital and parental responsibility and prevent the continued erosion of the family. Some of these proposals, as the

---

*It is interesting that the subject of the family has received far less attention in Europe, where both the sexual revolution and the subversion of the traditional family have gone much further than in the United States. To a certain extent the welfare state has so far masked some of the effects of these developments. But the welfare system itself is now extremely vulnerable, challenged by both the European Union and the global economy. In any case, the implications and consequences of this revolution would seem to call for more serious study than they have so far received in Europe (except for England, where they have been the subject of much attention and concern).

next chapter suggests, require the intervention of government: the revision, perhaps, of the no-fault divorce law to make divorce more difficult, or of the tax code to favor married couples, or of the welfare system to discourage single-parenthood, or of the education system to permit parents to exercise more judgment and responsibility for their children.

Apart from the specific, practical benefits of such reforms, they might also help create a moral climate more conducive to a healthy family, where motherhood and domesticity are as respectable a calling as the profession of law or the practice of business; fatherhood (present, not absent, fatherhood) is identified with manhood; sexual promiscuity is as socially unacceptable as smoking; the "bourgeois" family is an object of esteem rather than derision; and the culture is not deluded by the familiar euphemisms that dignify out-of-wedlock birth as an "alternative mode of parenting," or cohabitation as a "relationship," or an unmarried mate as a "significant other." Such a change in the ethos would help restore not only the integrity of the family but also that of the civil society in which it plays so vital a role.

CHAPTER IV

THE LAW AND POLITY:

"LEGISLATING MORALITY"

In his Godkin lectures at Harvard in 1986, Senator Daniel Patrick Moynihan observed: "The central conservative truth is that it is culture, not politics, that determines the success of a society. The central liberal truth is that politics can change a culture and save it from itself."[1] The essence of that dictum, the importance of culture and the relationship of culture to politics, is as true today as it has always been—and true of culture in the largest sense, the moral culture, the ethos of the country. But the primacy of culture for the conservative, and of politics for the liberal, has not always been evident.

It was, after all, the liberal (or radical) Thomas Paine who denigrated politics in his famous statement: "Society is produced by our wants, and government by our wickedness."*[2] And it was the conservative Edmund Burke who countered, in defense of politics: "Government is a contrivance of human

---

*But even Paine conceded some utility to government: ". . . the former [society] promotes our happiness positively by uniting our affections, the latter [government] negatively by restraining our vices." At its best, he added, government is a "necessary evil," at its worst an "intolerable one."

wisdom to provide for human wants."[3] Indeed, Burke went so far as to give the state (not society, as a common misquotation has it) "a partnership in all science; a partnership in all art; a partnership in every virtue, and in all perfection . . . a partnership not only between those who are living, but between those who are living, those who are dead, and those who are to be born."[4] Even John Stuart Mill (not the Mill of *On Liberty*, to be sure, but the Mill of *Representative Government*) said that "the most important point of excellence which any form of government can possess is to promote the virtue and intelligence of the people themselves."[5]

It is civil society, as opposed to government, that is generally assumed to be the bearer of the culture. But the early progenitors of the idea of civil society invoked it as the antithesis not of government but of the state of nature. John Locke, after explaining that "it is easy to discern who, and who are not, in political society together," made "political society" and "civil society" very nearly synonymous: "Those who are united into one body and have a common established law and judicature to appeal to, with authority to decide controversies between them and punish offenders, are in civil society one with another; but those who have no such common appeal, I mean on earth, are still in the state of nature." Thus offenses committed in the "commonwealth" are subject to the "legislative and executive power of civil society."[6]

Even Tocqueville did not distinguish as sharply between the civil and political realms as is generally thought. Nor did he give the primacy to civil society that is commonly attributed to him. On the contrary, he thought of the two spheres as intimately related, the one dependent upon the other. His concept of "associations" embraced "political associations" as much as "civil associations." And he saw "civil government" as a vital part of American democracy.[7] In one instance where he used the term "civil society," he did so in the chapter entitled "What are the Real Advantages which American Society Derives from a Democratic Government"—one of these advantages being the stimulating effect that democratic government has on society. Impressed by the extraordinary degree of political activity in the United States ("even the women often go to public meetings and forget household cares while they listen to political speeches"), he explained that the "constantly renewed agitation introduced by democratic government into political life passes, then, into civil society." Democracy might not be the most skillful of governments, but it does that which the most skillful cannot do: "It spreads throughout the body social a restless activity, superabundant force, and energy never found elsewhere."[8]

Moreover, it was political associations that were the inspiring force for civil associations.

> In all countries where political associations are forbidden, civil associations are rare. . . . Thus civil associations pave the way for political ones, but on the other hand, the art of political association singularly develops and improves this technique for civil purposes. . . . In this way politics spread a general habit and taste for association. . . . So one may think of political association as great free schools to which all citizens come to be taught the general theory of association.
>
> . . . .
>
> It is through political associations that Americans of every station, outlook, and age day by day acquire a general taste for association and get familiar with the way to use the same. Through them large numbers see, speak, listen, and stimulate each other to carry out all sorts of undertakings in common. Then they carry these conceptions with them into the affairs of civil life and put them to a thousand uses.[9]

. . .

What Americans have discovered since Tocqueville's day is that, for good or bad, government, law, and the other agencies of the state are as much the repositories, transmitters, even the creators of values as are the culture and the institutions of civil society. Legislation, judicial decisions, administrative regulations, penal codes, even tax codes are all, to one degree or another, instruments of moral legitimization—or illegitimization. One may say that legislators, judges, administrators, police officers, and agents of the Internal Revenue Service are not, and should not presume to be, moralists. That is what we pay preachers and teachers to do. In this postmodern world, however, preachers and teachers have all too often abdicated that role, which public officials, however unwittingly, have perforce assumed. Thus we hear this or that act of legislation acclaimed as a means for the promotion of "family values," "social justice," "equity," or "fairness."

Just as civil society may be appealed to as a democratic remedy for the diseases incident to democratic society, so a democratic polity may be invoked for the same purpose. One political remedy looks to the most democratic branch of the government, the legislature, to pass laws designed to promote the moral well-being of the country (legislation, for example, forbidding discrimination), or to revise those laws that have contributed to our ill-being (income tax measures discouraging marriage).* Another remedy is the transfer of power from the federal government to state and local governments, on the theory that the latter reflect the temper of the people more faithfully than does the remote Washington bureaucracy; this is the rationale behind the welfare reform that makes the states

---

*"The Project for American Renewal," sponsored by Senator Dan Coats, who is an enthusiastic proponent of civil society, contains eighteen specific proposals to remedy one or another social problem, in most cases by encouraging private, voluntary, communal efforts. All of them require legislation to initiate and implement them.[10]

responsible for relief. A more radical remedy looks to the Constitution for redress, such as an amendment to restore the right to prayer in the schools. These particular remedies may or may not be the best ways of addressing these particular problems. But they are not, in principle, ruled out on the grounds that they are political remedies, therefore inappropriate for moral problems.

It is often said that we cannot legislate morality. Yet we are constantly doing just that. The most dramatic example is the civil rights legislation of the 1960s, which illegitimized— morally as well as legally—racist conduct. But if laws can illegitimize certain kinds of behavior, they can legitimize others. The welfare system, for example, by subsidizing out-of-wedlock births, implicitly legitimizes such births. Or local ordinances requiring a school to distribute condoms may be said to legitimize promiscuity. Or the no-fault divorce law, by de-stigmatizing divorce, legitimizes it. William Galston, the political scientist and former domestic policy advisor to President Clinton, has observed: "Law can change incentives, and incentives can shape behavior. It is amazing how many people who believe (rightly) that civil rights laws helped change racial attitudes deny that any such consequences can flow from changes in the laws of marriage and divorce."[11]

In fact, law and government—good laws and judicious government—legitimize civil society itself. They are the preconditions of society, as they also are of democracy, providing the necessary framework and safeguarding the space within which individuals, families, communities, churches, and voluntary associations can effectively function.

This is why the state as well as society is so concerned with issues of crime and punishment. Crime is not only an aggression against individuals; it is an aggression against communities. Communities cannot flourish in the presence of lawlessness.

And it is lawlessness on the smallest as well as the largest scale that undermines communities—the kind of lawlessness that exhibits itself in graffiti in subways, or obstreperous panhandling in the streets, or booming radios in the parks, or the vandalizing of elevators in housing projects, or the presence of pornography bookstores in residential neighborhoods. ("Adult bookstores," the euphemism has it—as if there is something uniquely adult, rather than pathetically juvenile, about pornography.) James Q. Wilson and George L. Kelling have dubbed this the "broken windows" theory of crime.[12] Where there are broken windows, there will be crime, because the broken windows generate an atmosphere of lawlessness that is conducive to crime. To be serious about promoting civil society, the government has to be serious about curbing crime. And to do that it has to proceed vigorously against the small as well as large transgressions of the law.*

In my youth, there was a saying, "There ought to be a law." And so there should be against these small but troublesome offenses against society. In fact, there are such laws. The problem is that all too often they are not enforced, partly because of the reluctance of the police to engage in the futile exercise of apprehending criminals who are then released by the courts, and partly because of the permissive attitude of some courts, which view such laws as infringements on civil liberties. (One judge has defended panhandling as "informative and persuasive speech.")[14] The failure to enforce the law may be even more

---

*Echoing the "broken windows" theory, John DiIulio proposes a "broken bottles" theory. Alcohol, even when it does not directly cause crime, acts as a "multiplier of crime," creating an environment in which crime, violence, and disorder are rampant. Citing the correlation between crime rates and liquor stores, DiIulio calls for restrictions on advertising and stricter zoning ordinances limiting the number of liquor stores.[13]

demoralizing to the community than the crime itself, for it brings a spirit of lawlessness into the very heart of the legal system.

Conversely, the enforcement of law—the visible, conspicuous evidence of enforcement—is as morally fortifying as the reduction of crime itself, not only because it makes individuals safer and communities more secure, but also because it signifies a reaffirmation of the law itself, a relegitimization, as it were, of the law. For many years, the dominant "progressive" ideology was so suspicious of the agencies and mechanisms of law enforcement that it belittled or disparaged the very idea of imprisonment. This ideology was somewhat muted when the rapid rise of criminality could no longer be explained away by the familiar arguments that the statistics merely reflected new modes of reporting or that they were the product of a racial bias (by exaggerating crimes committed by blacks). But the antipathy to the very idea of imprisonment still survives in the media, so that an official report demonstrating a significant decline of crime is featured in the *New York Times* under the heading, "Even as Crime Falls, Inmates Increase"[15]—as if the incarceration of criminals has nothing to do with the decline of crime, as if, indeed, there is something paradoxical in the inverse relationship between those two figures.

There is no doubt that the dramatic reduction in the incidence of crime in New York City is at least partly the result of a deliberate and concerted effort to prosecute minor as well as major violators of the law—youths who jump the turnstiles to avoid paying the subway fare, or squeegee men who exercise their peculiar mode of extortion on motorists, or bicyclists who ignore the lights, or even jaywalkers. Such prosecutions not only have a salutary effect on the quality of life in the city; they also send a message about the gravity of the law itself—of any law—which carries over into more serious crimes. (As an additional bonus, they sometimes lead to the exposure and prosecution of more serious crimes; turnstile jumpers sometimes turn out to be carrying illegal weapons or fleeing from the scene of a crime.) The most obvious functions of the law are deterrence and punishment. But it has an additional purpose that is too often slighted today. Properly conceived and executed, the law also serves as a reaffirmation, a validation, of the moral sense of society, the natural, legitimate desire for just retribution. If the agencies of the law fail to perform that function, if they do not punish lawbreakers—and punish them appropriately, commensurately with their crimes—they invite a contempt and recklessness that are an invitation to vigilantism. Citizens will take the law in their own hands, if the law itself defaults on its duties and responsibilities. And vigilantism is a form of lawlessness, of criminality; in the guise of protecting society, it violates those laws that are the foundations of society.

"Properly conceived and executed"—that is the rub. Today there is much about the law that is improper—not only the failure of enforcement but the invocation of the law for trivial and unworthy purposes. The litigious temper of the times is a consequence of the decline of civility and the concomitant proliferation of "rights"—legal rights in place of the manners and morals that once arbitrated disagreements and disputes. In this sense the law has become not so much the aid and abettor of manners and morals as a substitute for them.

Machiavelli described the relation of manners to the law: "For as good manners cannot subsist without good laws, so those laws cannot be put into execution without good manners."[16] Hobbes went on to explain that manners meant something more than "small morals" (what we now call "etiquette"): "By manners I mean not here, decency of behavior; as how one man should salute another, or how a man should wash his mouth, or pick his teeth before company, and such other points of the *small morals*; but those qualities of mankind, that concern their living together in peace and unity."[17] Burke went further, insisting upon the relation of manners and morals not only to the law but to liberty as well.

> Manners are of more importance than laws. Upon them, in a great measure, the laws depend. The law touches us but here and there, and now and then. Manners are what vex or soothe, corrupt or purify, exalt or debase, barbarize or refine us, by a constant, steady, uniform, insensible operation, like that of the air we breathe in. They give their whole form and colour to our lives. According to their quality, they aid morals, they supply them, or they totally destroy them.[18]
>
> . . . Men are qualified for civil liberty in exact proportion to their disposition to put moral chains upon their own appetites. . . . Society cannot exist unless a controlling power upon will and appetite be placed somewhere, and the less of it there is within, the more there must be without.[19]

Until quite recently, society has taken for granted the continuum of manners and morals ("small morals" and large), and of both with the law. It was understood that the law did not create or transcend manners and morals; on the contrary, it derived from them and reflected them. Indeed, it relied upon them for its own efficacy. Today, in the absence of any firm sense of manners and morals, the law has become the only recognized authority. Just as the state often acts as a surrogate for the dysfunctional family, so the law is a surrogate for a dysfunctional culture and ethos. This litigious disposition is aggravated by other circumstances, such as the inflated regulatory system that presumes to micromanage individual and corporate behavior, or the passion for "political correctness" that preoccupies the governing bodies of universities. To all the other "diseases of democracy" we may now add the mania for litigation.[20]

As the law has become more intrusive, so has the judiciary.

The vagaries of so many judicial decisions at the lower levels have been more than matched by the imperiousness of other decisions at the highest levels—the "judicial oligarchy," as Judge Robert Bork has characterized the Supreme Court.[21] Under the title "The End of Democracy?" the journal *First Things* has posed the question, "Whether we have reached or are reaching the point where conscientious citizens can no longer give moral assent to the existing regime." Assuring their readers that the question is "in no way hyperbolic," the editors insist that the "judicial usurpation of power" on the part of state courts and, more perilously, the Supreme Court has resulted in a grave "crisis of legitimacy."[22] The crisis is exemplified by the courts' rulings on abortion and euthanasia, which are said to violate both the Constitution and the moral law. But these cases only dramatize the more fundamental issue: the abandonment by the Supreme Court of a strictly constitutional principle of interpretation and the arrogation to the judiciary of powers properly belonging to the legislative branch of government.

Some commentators (myself included) have argued that *First Things* was indeed hyperbolic in posing the question as it did. But the journal did strike a chord, as is evident from the wide-ranging controversy it provoked.[23] And the issue goes beyond the Supreme Court to a multitude of lesser cases decided by the lower courts, which often seem eccentric and arbitrary. In this respect, the Supreme Court serves as a dubious model for the lower courts, for if the justices can be so negligent of the founding document of the Republic, judges may feel justified in indulging their own caprices.

The law, we are discovering, is too serious a matter to be left to lawyers or even judges. We are beginning to understand how to use the law to protect ourselves against criminals and depredators. We have yet to learn how to protect ourselves against some of the practitioners of the law itself. Yet the troubling experience of recent years is no reason to question the legitimacy of either the law or the "regime." On the contrary, it is more reason than ever to assert the necessity and legitimacy, if also the vulnerability and frailty, of both. Just as there is a reciprocal relationship between civil society and the state, each depending upon the other for its effective functioning, so there is an integral connection between the law and the ethos of society. Neither can sustain itself without the other.

"There ought to be a law" recalls another adage from my youth: "Don't make a federal case out of it." The two neatly supplement each other, for they remind us that while we need laws, they should be, as much as possible, state and local laws rather than federal (that is, national) ones. Scholars have a fancy name for this, "subsidiarity": the highest or central authority should have a subsidiary or secondary function, performing only those tasks that cannot be effectively dealt with by lesser or local authorities. This principle is implicitly affirmed by surveys showing that the level of popular satisfaction with government is in inverse proportion to the level of government itself. Only one-third of the people, in one poll, expressed "a great deal" or "quite a lot" of confidence in the federal government, somewhat more than that in state government, and over half in local government.[24]

For much of the history of this country, most laws were local rather than national. Pornography, for example, used to be entirely a matter of local concern; the formula governing its regulation was "community standards." It was only after World War I, when the federal government attempted to control the distribution of pornography, that it became a contentious issue and, ultimately, a lost cause, hopelessly mired in constitutional controversies. Similarly, abortion, until *Roe v. Wade,* was left to the jurisdiction of the states, where it occasioned some controversy but not nearly as much as when the Supreme Court established a uniform national policy.

The welfare reform act of 1996 is the most dramatic assertion of subsidiarity—"devolution," as we now call it.* In this case, subsidiarity has an additional function, for what seems on the surface to be merely an administrative change, the transfer of welfare to the states, carries with it a profound change of principle. Indeed, the administrative change itself may be of secondary importance.[25] The more momentous result is the abandonment of the principle of welfare as a national entitlement, a "right." This means that welfare no longer has the legal status it once had, and, more significantly, that it is deprived of the moral status that comes with that legal right.

Before the recent reform, there had been much talk of a "welfare crisis," but this was a misnomer. There was no welfare crisis. There was, however, a moral crisis. The United States is a rich and a compassionate country. It can afford to sustain a large population on welfare, and has in fact done so for decades. What it cannot afford is a large demoralized population that exhibits all the symptoms of the social pathology associated with welfare dependency—broken families, crime, school dropouts. Welfare dependency is not the primary cause of that pathology, but it is an important factor in it.

The system of relief was less than two years old when its initiator, President Franklin Roosevelt, cautioned Americans against an excessive reliance upon it: "Continued dependence upon relief induces a spiritual and moral disintegration fundamentally destructive to the national fiber. To dole out relief in this way is to administer a narcotic, a subtle destroyer of the human spirit."[26] Roosevelt's relief program was, in fact, modest. But President Lyndon Johnson's "Great Society" and "War Against Poverty" were not. It took another liberal, Robert F. Kennedy, to point out that this new mode of welfare unwit-

*"Devolution" has become part of the political vocabulary in America only recently; "federalism" is more commonly used to refer to the transfer of power to the states. In England "devolution" has long been familiar to denote home rule, for Scotland most notably.

tingly degraded those it meant to help. In 1966 he discovered what many liberals were to take much longer to learn.

Opponents of welfare have always said that welfare is degrading, both to the giver and the recipient. They have said that it destroys self-respect, that it lowers incentives, that it is contrary to American ideals.

Most of us deprecated and disregarded these criticisms. People were in need; obviously, we felt, to help people in trouble was the right thing to do.

But in our urge to help, we also disregarded elementary fact. For the criticisms of welfare do have a center of truth, and they are confirmed by the evidence.

Recent studies have shown, for example, that higher welfare payments often encourage students to drop out of school, that they encourage families to disintegrate, and that they often lead to lifelong dependency.[27]

. . .

Since President Johnson's time, the system of welfare has expanded enormously, and with it the unfortunate effects Kennedy observed. Conceived originally as a temporary recourse in time of need, welfare became, for part of the population, a long-term means of subsistence, a way of life, a "culture of dependency" transmitted from generation to generation. The very word "dependency" is suggestive. The older "work ethic" did more than make a virtue of work. It also made a virtue of independence, and that carried with it other virtues: responsibility, prudence, self-discipline. A culture of dependency is inimical to these virtues because it demoralizes not only the individual but also the family. As the state becomes the chief provider, the father is reduced to the role of procreator, the husband becomes dispensable, and the family, often reduced to one parent, becomes impoverished and unstable.

There is a school of thought that emphasizes the economic incentives that brought so many people onto the welfare rolls—

cash, food stamps, housing allowances, medical benefits, and the like, often adding up to more than the earnings of a low-wage worker. By the same token, the economic disincentives in the recent reform—the reduction or withdrawal of some of these benefits—have been credited with removing a great many people from the rolls. These disincentives are undoubtedly important. But no less so are the moral disincentives implicit in the reform. Such provisions as work in return for welfare, a time limit for recipients of welfare, the requirement that teenage mothers receive welfare only in their parents' homes or in residences for unmarried mothers, or a "family cap" denying additional benefits for new births to mothers already on welfare, send out the message that chronic dependency is no longer regarded as morally or socially acceptable. They reaffirm what was once derided (in some circles is still derided) as the "Puritan ethic" or "work ethic."

For the first time since the 1970s the number of people on welfare has dropped below ten million. In 1998 it was 8.3 million, a decline of more than a third in five years, and of over a fourth in the two years since the passage of the new law.[28] If much of that decrease (more than 40 percent, according to the President's Council of Economic Advisers) reflects the booming economy, more than 30 percent, it is estimated, can be attributed to the reform itself—and to the anticipation of the reform.[29] There is also impressionistic evidence that at least part of this decline is the result not so much of the more stringent provisions of the state laws as of the change in the moral climate. Newspapers not notably sympathetic to the reform have featured interviews with women currently or formerly on welfare who express their approval of the "workfare" system (welfare given upon condition of service, usually on public projects). Workfare, they say, is personally more satisfying than welfare and independent employment is more satisfactory still—this even in cases where the net income from working is less than it would be from welfare. Speaking of the pride, the sense of independence and dignity, they get from working and being self-supporting, these women are, in effect, beginning to internalize the social norms that are implicit in the new law.

Critics of the reform were at first quick to point out that the decline in welfare had not been accompanied by a reduction of out-of-wedlock births and that it may have been responsible for an increase in the number of abortions. In fact, both out-of-wedlock births and abortions have dropped, although the causal relation with welfare has not been statistically established. What is clear, however, is that attitudes toward out-of-wedlock births and casual sex are beginning to change. According to a poll in New Jersey, which has a family cap policy, two-thirds of the women on welfare say that the policy is fair and four-fifths praise it for promoting responsibility.[30] "They should have done this a long time ago," reports one woman whose workfare job is picking up trash in the park. "If they had, there wouldn't be children having children. Maybe if they knew they had to come to work every morning, it would make them more ambitious."[31]

The welfare system itself, it is important to remember, has not been abolished; indeed, it still enjoys the considerable financial support of the federal as well as the state governments. Nor is it expected that welfare dependency will ever be eliminated; there will always be individuals and families in need of temporary or permanent relief. Nor has the cost of welfare declined as much as might have been expected; in some cases the drop in the relief rolls has been achieved only at the cost of a rise in expenditures incurred to facilitate the transition to employment. The success of the reform, most of its proponents agree, will be measured not in monetary but in moral terms, in the principle learned by Robert Kennedy thirty years earlier: "that what is given or granted can be taken away, that what is begged can be refused; but what is earned is kept, that what is self-made is inalienable, that what you do for yourselves and for your children can never be taken away."[32]

. . .

The decline of the welfare rolls, like that of the incidence of crime, reminds us once again that there is no such thing as "value-free" social policies or government actions, that such policies and actions are almost always infused, for good or bad, with moral content, and that today, more than ever, as social problems become more exigent, we cannot afford the luxury of being apolitical, of depriving ourselves of the proper resources of government and law. Civil society itself is dependent upon the judicious use of law and government, if only to preserve and strengthen its constituent parts. Thus a sensible tax policy can encourage two-parent families, as it presently encourages home-ownership. Or divorce laws can be devised to deter the breakup of the family, rather than, as at present, facilitating it. Or the courts can once again support, as they did for most of our history, the rights of communities to enforce anti-pornography and anti-obscenity ordinances. Or the government can induce private philanthropy, by means of fiscal and other incentives, to devote more of their resources to the needy, thus complementing the public "safety net" with the kinds of services that only private charities can provide.*

One courageous analyst of social problems and policies has revived the once derogatory term "paternalism" to describe what both public and private agencies do and what they should more effectively attempt to do. Such paternalism, Lawrence Mead explains, is evident in the work provisions of the welfare reform, or the rules set by shelters for the homeless, or the educational standards in public schools, or the tests administered to addicts in

---

*Critics of private philanthropy point out that it acquired its good name (and, perhaps, its tax exemption) when it was principally concerned with helping the poor. Today, by far the bulk of its resources go to religious institutions, as well as education, the arts, and environmental causes.

drug rehabilitation programs, or the monitoring of offenders on probation and parole. In each case, the purpose is to encourage and enforce desirable kinds of behavior. Both conservatives and liberals, for different reasons, Mead points out, have been ambivalent about this kind of paternalism. Conservatives approve of the idea that the recipients of help be obliged to help themselves, but deplore the role of government in providing that help; and liberals welcome the enhanced role of government for the purpose of rehabilitation, but are suspicious of the "blame the victim" undertone of this policy. Eventually, Mead concludes, social sanctions may take the place of governmental ones, but at present some forms of paternalism are the only means of coping with the behavioral disorders of a dependent and dysfunctional population.[33]

What is evident in the rethinking that has been going on about social problems and policies in recent years is the bankruptcy of the theories and practices that have prevailed for the past half-century or more. Just as nineteenth-century reformers consciously sought to fashion social policies in accord with moral objectives, so their successors tried, just as consciously, to divorce social policies from any suspicion of morality. In part, this reflects the assumption that society is responsible for all social problems and therefore has the task of solving them, and in part the prevailing spirit of relativism, which finds it distasteful to pass moral judgments upon others, let alone impose moral conditions upon them. After decades of cultivating such a "nonjudgmental" philosophy, we are beginning to discover that all policies, for good or ill, have moral consequences, and that only by deliberately devising policies in accord with desirable ends can the good outweigh the bad.

We are also discovering that the best-intentioned policies are subject to the inexorable law of social affairs: the law of unintended consequences. Charles Murray has subjected to the scrutiny of that law one such proposal, the bill to give tax credits to mothers who stay at home to care for their children. This bill has the commendable aim of strengthening the family by encouraging home care, thus counterbalancing the subsidies for day care that sometimes have the opposite effect. But because the tax credit is relatively small, Murray points out, it would favor more affluent families for whom the credit would be an agreeable bonus, without serving as a serious financial incentive for poorer mothers to stay at home. It would also undermine the workfare provision of welfare, for if married mothers are encouraged to stay at home, surely unmarried ones should be as well. But the most serious defect of the bill, Murray maintains, would be the creation of yet another entitlement which, like all previous ones, would snowball far beyond its original scope, making the government a co-partner of the family, thus vitiating the purpose of the bill by eroding the sense of parental responsibility.[34]

Applied rigorously, the law of unintended consequences would have a paralyzing effect on any attempt of the government to remedy any disorder of society. For a libertarian, this is indeed the lesson to be drawn from that law. Yet the disorder is there, and may be serious enough to risk whatever unintended consequences may follow. Moreover, the reform itself might have an immediate positive result that would override its future unintended effects. The tax credit, for example, would send a message to the public that home care, if at all possible, is preferable to day care and that society is appreciative and respectful of stay-at-home mothers. In a culture that tends to value careers for women more than domesticity, the tax credit might help restore the moral status both of full-time motherhood and of the two-parent family.

Other social policies, devised with the best intentions, might similarly be faulted for their unintended consequences. The "covenant marriage" in Louisiana, permitting couples to subscribe voluntarily to a more binding contract than the official one, is an attempt to correct the excesses of the no-fault divorce law. But the very existence of that alternative may have the unwitting effect of further weakening marriage by making the more customary marital rite look like an open invitation to divorce. And even for those who do adopt the covenant, the requirement of premarital counseling may induce a premature sense of doubt and uncertainty, a blight upon what should be a confident, romantic, unequivocal commitment. Its supporters, however, can plausibly argue that these unfortunate by-products of the covenant are offset by its considerable merits. At a time when divorce is so commonplace, the reaffirmation of an older, stricter form of marriage is no mean achievement.*

Almost any action of government may be subject to the same kinds of equivocal effects. But so may non-actions of the government. If it is well to be reminded of the unintended consequences of the best-intentioned laws, we should also keep in mind the unintended consequences of laws not passed, of reforms not made.

The arguments against "big government" are well taken, but they should not translate into arguments against law or government per se—the prudent exercise of legislation, administration, and adjudication. When conservatives object to the use of government for social or moral purposes, it is often a particular

---

*Another proposal to deter divorce has less to be said in its favor. This is the "marriage commitment fund," according to which a fixed percentage of a couple's income would be set aside each year to serve as an annuity in old age if the couple remains married or to be distributed to the children if the couple should divorce.[35] This has the disadvantage of all prenuptial agreements, of being so calculating and materialistic as to create an initial skepticism about the marriage itself and ultimately to undermine the moral, to say nothing of the spiritual or romantic, meaning of marriage.

kind of government they have in mind, most notably, the welfare state. And when they object to the welfare state, it is on the grounds that it is big government. But a no less important objection is that it is bad government. The English, who have had more experience with it than we have, call it the "nanny state," a state that treats individuals not as adults but as wayward and improvident children who require constant supervision and protection by their guardians. More recently it has been dubbed the "therapeutic state," catering (or pandering) to the supposed emotional and psychic needs of the citizens.[36]

The inefficiency and high cost of such a state, and its unlimited tendency to expand, are the least of its vices. A more serious objection is that it is demeaning and demoralizing to those who come under its not-too-tender embrace. In reaction to this kind of state, civil society is often invoked, in the hope that there, in the intimate, personal relations of daily life, individuals will be able to function as free, responsible, moral human beings. Released from the tutelage of the government, secure in the natural institutions of civil society, people will care for themselves and for each other, provide for their needs and amenities, enjoy all the rights and duties of full-fledged adults.

In their eagerness to do away with the nanny state, however, some conservatives risk belittling, even delegitimizing, the state itself. It is a delicate balancing act that is required: to reconstruct or diminish the welfare state while retaining a healthy respect for the state itself and for its ancillary institutions. (Critics of the Nixon and Clinton administrations have had a similar problem: to expose the infractions of the President without detracting from the dignity and legitimacy of the presidency itself.) One of the unfortunate consequences of the welfare state is that it has exacerbated the anarchic impulse in American society. The bureaucratic zealots of the left give a semblance of plausibility to the armed fanatics of the right. Today, more than ever, when there are so many legitimate grievances against government, Americans cannot afford to illegitimize legitimate government.

In denigrating the state, we also risk attenuating the idea of citizenship. The inhabitants of civil society are just that—inhabitants of families and communities, churches and voluntary associations, workplaces and marketplaces. Citizenship thus becomes equated with civility and sociability. Good citizens are good neighbors. They attend PTA meetings, donate blood, curb their dogs, are courteous and considerate. These are no mean virtues. In our time, they are very considerable virtues. But they are not the only or the most important virtues associated with citizenship.

Citizenship, in the classic sense, is a political concept. The citizen (*civis*) was a member of the *civitas*, which signified not so much a place of residence as the primary political unit. Until very recently citizenship retained this essentially political meaning. It involved an active participation in the political process—voting, officeholding, collective decision-making—as well as the more passive function of obeying the laws, paying taxes, and otherwise fulfilling one's obligations to the state. Citizenship in this sense has a special significance in the United States, where it has served to assimilate waves of immigrants from totally different ethnic and social backgrounds, giving them a common role, a common status, and a common stake in the country. Think what it meant to Jewish immigrants from Tsarist Russia (I have in mind my own parents) to obtain American citizenship, to become fully accredited members of a political community—and a democratic community at that.

Or think what it meant to the working classes in Western countries when they finally acquired the franchise of which they had been so long deprived. When the Chartists, the English working-class radicals in the late 1830s and '40s, demanded the vote, it was not to improve their economic or material conditions. If this had been their purpose, they would have formed trade unions or socialist parties or at the very least agitated for minimum wages and factory reforms. Instead, all the Six Points of the Charter were political: the suffrage, annual elections, secret ballot, etc. Their demands were political because political equality—not economic or social equality, they did not expect or even aspire to that—was seen as the essential requisite of civic and moral equality, the recognition of their status as fully responsible members of society. It was for this reason, because they put so high a premium on citizenship in the political sense, that they consciously set out to become morally and intellectually worthy of it. Thus the "Temperance Chartists" took the vow of teetotalism, while the "Education Chartists" organized reading and learning groups—temperance and education being the virtues they believed to be the essential qualifications for citizenship. In seeking to be admitted as full and equal members of the polity, they were testifying to their desire to be regarded as fully human.

Aristotle reminds us that "man is by nature a political animal." Not a "social animal," as this is often mistranslated.* It is not in the household or in the village, Aristotle says, but only in the *polis* that man is truly human, decisively different from "bees or any other gregarious animals."[38] Bees and animals, after all, also inhabit households and villages (civil society, we would now say). They provide shelter and sustenance for themselves and their young; they even have social relations and social structures. What they do not have is a polity, a government of laws and institutions. Only men are political because only they are rational. And only in the polity can they rationally, consciously try to establish a just regime and pursue the good life.

---

*This is an ancient, not a modern, corruption. Hannah Arendt points out that it was Seneca who mistranslated Aristotle's "political animal" as "social animal" and that Aquinas perpetuated it in his famous dictum, "Man is by nature political, that is, social."[37]

. . .

To reduce citizenship to the modern idea of civility, the good-neighbor idea, is to belittle not only the political role of the citizen but also the virtues expected of the citizen—the "civic virtues," as they were known in antiquity and in early republican thought. It is these virtues Aristotle had in mind when he wrote that the good citizen "should know how to govern like a freeman, and how to obey like a freeman—these are the virtues of a citizen."[39] Or Montesquieu, when he made "virtue" the distinctive principle of republican government: "It is not a moral, nor a Christian, but a political virtue; and it is the spring which sets the republican government in motion, as honor is the spring which gives motion to monarchy. Hence it is that I have distinguished the love of one's country, and of equality, by the appellation of political virtue."[40] Even the Founding Fathers, seeking to create a constitution that would depend on a plurality of interests rather than simply the exercise of virtue, believed that civic virtue—the self-control and self-discipline required for self-government—was an essential attribute both of those who govern the republic and of those who are governed.

The displacement of "civic virtue" by "civility" has been accompanied by a shift from what has been called the "vigorous" virtues to the "caring" virtues. The vigorous virtues include courage, ambition, adventurousness, audacity, creativity; the caring virtues are respect, trustworthiness, compassion, fairness, decency.[41] The two kinds of virtues are not mutually exclusive, for they pertain to different aspects of life. The caring virtues make for good families and friends, neighbors and associates; they render daily life, life in civil society, livable and agreeable. Especially in the present condition of society, these are altogether admirable attributes. But they do not preclude others that should command our respect—those vigorous, outsized, heroic virtues that transcend family and community and may even, on occasion, violate the conventions of civility. These are the virtues that characterize great leaders, although not necessarily good friends.

If citizenship is demeaned by the habit of "thinking small," of focusing entirely on the goods and needs of daily life, so is leadership. Presidential candidates for the year 2000 have defined themselves by a succession of campaign slogans and issues befitting, as has been pointed out, the mayor of a small town rather than aspirants for the presidency of the United States. Thus Vice-President Gore has addressed himself, at some length, to such subjects as traffic congestion, the cow manure that pollutes streams, over-the-counter drug labels, computers in the school room, and an "Airline Passenger Bill of Rights" to compensate passengers, among other things, for lost baggage; while another contender, Elizabeth Dole, the former Secretary of Transportation, prides herself on her proposal to install emergency aisle safety lights on airplanes.

Another candidate, the former senator Bill Bradley, urges us to rebuild civil society rather than look for national heroes to solve our problems. He quotes a character in Bertolt Brecht's *Galileo*, "Pity the nation that has no heroes," to which Galileo responds, "Pity the nation that needs them."[42] The senator evidently shares Galileo's sentiments (or Brecht's, which is not quite the same thing). In the wake of recent Washington scandals, so, apparently, do a fair number of people. Presidents once figured prominently among the nation's heroes. That is no longer the case. Schoolteachers report that in their discussions with students, they "downsize" the conception of the hero. One teacher, explaining that she herself has seen her own heroes fail in recent years, says that when she asks students to identify heroes, she points them to "ordinary heroes, folks who do good works in the community."[43]

This domesticating or downgrading of the hero is a sad commentary on contemporary life. It is a denial of the very idea of the heroic, of the person who, by definition, is something more than "ordinary," who does great deeds rather than merely "good works." It is also an affront to ordinary people who do not themselves aspire to greatness and heroism but who are impoverished by a culture that is suspicious of these qualities. Hegel, who is better known for his praise of "world-historical individuals," appreciated the need of ordinary citizens for a spirit that elevates them above their ordinary lives. In civil society, he said, individuals begin to overcome their "particularity" by experiencing themselves as more than isolated individuals. But it is in the state that they truly fulfill themselves, for it is there that they transcend their particularity by being identified with something larger than themselves, with the "Spirit" or "Idea" manifest in the state.[44]

Americans have never been comfortable with such terms as "Spirit" or "Idea," especially as applied to the state. But we do understand and respect the ideas of patriotism and heroism. And our wisest statesmen have understood that inspiring such ideas is an important part of their mission. As George Will has memorably put it: "Statecraft" is a form of "Soulcraft"; it helps shape the character, and hence the soul, of a people.[45] Of a people, not merely of individuals. And not merely the character of a people but its very identity, the sense of nationality and high purpose that engenders a worthy patriotism.

This, finally, is what we are in danger of losing today. It is natural and commendable for individuals to seek their satisfaction in their families and communities, to make them the center of their emotional ties and moral commitments. But to feel completely fulfilled in those roles and entirely identified with them is to lose that larger identity and aspiration that come not from civil society but from the polity. Today, when politics has been so tainted by cynicism and scandal, the retreat to private and communal life is all too understandable. But it would be most unfortunate if the state were deprived, in peacetime and more urgently in wartime, of the enthusiastic service and loyalty of its citizens. Why concern oneself with public affairs, with matters remote from one's immediate interests, if one's commitments are entirely familial and local? Why compete for national office in Washington if all one's values and aspirations are centered on one's family and community? Why, in times of national emergency, take up arms and possibly give up one's life if one has so tenuous a relationship to the country as a whole—if there is so little sense of a national identity requiring that ultimate sacrifice?

Edmund Burke's "little platoon" is a maxim often invoked in discussions of civil society. But the context of that phrase is rarely quoted.

> To be attached to the subdivision, to love the little platoon we belong to in society, is the first principle (the germ as it were) of public affections. It is the first link in the series by which we proceed towards a love to our country and to mankind.[46]

And again:

> We begin our public affections in our families. . . . We pass on to our neighborhoods and our habitual provincial connections. These are inns and resting places. . . . Perhaps it is a sort of elemental training to those higher and more large regards, by which alone men come to be affected, as with their own concern, in the prosperity of a kingdom.[47]

Civil society, Burke teaches us, is a two-way street. It takes us back to our roots, to our nearest and dearest. But it should also take us forward to our nation and country. It recalls us to the "love of one's country" that Montesquieu regarded as the distinguishing virtue of a republic—a virtue that elevates us, that invests our daily life, and civil society itself, with a larger meaning, that dignifies the individual even as it humanizes politics.

CHAPTER V
RELIGION: "THE FIRST OF THEIR POLITICAL INSTITUTIONS"

Like civil society, the polity and the law are necessary but not sufficient remedies for the disorders of society. Even as the Founding Fathers devised their "new science of politics" based upon the principle of divided powers and interests, they understood that that "science" alone cannot sustain a proper republican government. Republican government means self-government—self-discipline, self-restraint, self-control, self-reliance—"republican virtue," in short. In the absence of such virtue the best political arrangements are of no avail. "I go on this great republican principle," James Madison said, "that the people will have virtue and intelligence to select men of virtue and wisdom. . . . To suppose that any form of government will secure liberty or happiness without any virtue in the people, is a chimerical idea."[1]

What the Founding Fathers also understood was that in a republic such virtue is intimately related to religion. However skeptical or deistic they may have been in their own beliefs, however determined they were to avoid anything like an established church, they had no doubt that religion is an essential part of the social order because it is a vital part of the moral order. "If men are so wicked as we now see them with religion," Benjamin Franklin said, "what would they be if without it?"[2] John Adams put it more tactfully: "Our constitution was made only for a moral and religious people. It is wholly inadequate to the government of any other."[3] And George Washington, in his Farewell Address, cautioned his countrymen not to "indulge the supposition that morality can be maintained without religion": "Of all the dispositions and habits which lead to political prosperity, religion and morality are indispensable supports." And then, as if to warn them that enlightenment was no substitute for religion, he added: "Whatever may be conceded to the influence of refined education on minds of peculiar structure, reason and experience both forbid us to expect that national morality can prevail in exclusion of religious principle."[4]

Even Thomas Jefferson, who was suspected of being a nonbeliever, believed in Christianity as the national faith. A recently discovered handwritten history of a Washington parish recounts his exchange with a friend who happened to meet him on his way to church one Sunday morning carrying his large red prayer book.

"You going to church Mr. J. You do not believe a word in it."

"Sir," said Jefferson, "no nation has ever yet existed or been governed without religion. Nor can be. The Christian religion is the best religion that has been given to man and I as chief Magistrate of this nation am bound to give it the sanction of my example. Good morning Sir."[5]

Tocqueville, visiting America a few decades later, found that a democracy, even more than a republic, requires something more than a sound polity to compensate for its twin disabilities: an egalitarianism that undermines liberty and an individualism that saps "the spring of public virtues."[6] The remedy generally ascribed to him is the voluntary associations identified with civil society. But other associations were no less important to him: the political associations that animate democratic government, and the religious associations, the churches, that keep alive a sense of public virtue.

"The religious atmosphere of the country," Tocqueville wrote, "was the first thing that struck me on arrival in the United States." Unlike France, where the Enlightenment had seen to it that religion and freedom were "almost always marching in opposite directions," in America they were "intimately linked together in joint reign over the same land."[7] It was religion in the service of virtue that made freedom possible. And American religion was uniquely able to do this because it was not an official, established religion. Americans cherished the idea of religious freedom, the separation of church and state, as much as they cherished their particular church or sect. Religion was "the first of their political institutions," precisely because it was not, strictly speaking, a political institution at all.[8]

Again and again Tocqueville reflected upon the relationship of religion to morality and of both to freedom and democracy:

> While the law allows the American people to do everything, there are things which religion prevents them from imagining and forbids them to dare.[9]

> Freedom sees religion as the companion of its struggles and triumphs, the cradle of its infancy, and the divine source of its rights. Religion is considered as the guardian of mores, and mores are regarded as the guarantee of the laws and pledge for the maintenance of freedom itself.[10]

> Despotism may be able to do without faith, but freedom cannot. Religion is much more needed in . . . [a] republic . . . than in . . . [a] monarchy . . . , and in democratic republics most of all. How could society escape destruction if, when political ties are relaxed, moral ties are not tightened? And what can be done with a people master of itself if it is not subject to God?[11]

Tocqueville anticipated the objection commonly heard today that this view of religion is demeaning, even irreligious, because it is concerned more with the utility of religion than with its spirituality. "I do not know," he admitted, "if all Americans have faith in their religion—for who can read the secrets of the heart?—but I am sure that they think it necessary for the maintenance of republican institutions."[12] Every religion, he noted, has two dimensions: one that elevates the soul above the material and sensory world, and the other that imposes upon each man an obligation to mankind. These are complementary functions, and both are essential for the self-government that is at the heart of liberty and democracy.[13]

Religion was integral to American democracy because the United States derived its Enlightenment not from France, which, as Tocqueville suggested, was antireligious and anticlerical (in large part because religion and the church were so intimately allied with a repressive monarchy), but from England, where even deists were tolerant of the established church. (David Hume, who was skeptical in matters of faith and fearful of religious passions, was a staunch supporter of the Church of England, if only because he saw Anglicanism as a corrective to zealotry.) Moreover, in England, as in the United States, religion was a democratizing as well as a liberalizing force. "The poor are the Christians," John Wesley proclaimed, taking upon himself the special mission of bringing the Gospel to them. When the Anglican churches were closed to him, he made a virtue out of necessity by preaching in the open fields to those who did not feel welcome in the established church. Wesley himself was no democrat, either in his political views or in relation to his own church. But the Wesleyan church structure—with "families" led by "fathers" and the members addressing each other as "brothers" and "sisters"—promoted a sense of fraternity and community that made them hospitable to the poor.[14]

When Wesley's associate, George Whitefield, made his sensational tours in America in the 1740s, he found himself in congenial territory, the democratic spirit of Methodism being in perfect accord with the other sects spawned by the Great Awakening. This spirit derived from a theology that declared all men to be sinners capable of achieving salvation through personal, spiritual conversion, and from an organizational structure that encouraged lay participation, itinerant preaching, and a sense of equality and community. Thus the revivalist sects appealed to the poor and not so poor, to blacks as well as whites, to people of all callings and aspirations.

Historians have debated the precise nature of the relationship between the Great Awakening and the American Revolution, but few doubt that the two were closely related.[15] Martin Marty speaks of two simultaneous revolutions, the first an inward, spiritual one that made American religion evangelical,* the second an outward, political one that made American society republican. Inspiring both revolutions, and linking the two, was a new kind of millenarianism that was gradual and optimistic rather than cataclysmic and apocalyptic, and that looked to America, the "city upon a hill," for the redemption that would usher in the "latter-day glory." At this point, Marty observes, "pious and Enlightenment ideas could meet, so the two schools of thought could employ one kind of futurist imagery while seeking separate goals: a Christian America or a republican America. Both were part of a common 'pursuit of happiness.'"[16]

This first Great Awakening was followed by others that were dignified by the same title. The Second Great Awakening, starting around the turn of the century and reaching its climax in the Civil War, rejected the more rigorous Calvinistic teachings

---

*American religion was theologically "evangelical" (with a lower-case "e"), not "Evangelical" (capitalized) in the English sense, where it had an institutional identity.

⌐of the earlier revival and had different social commitments: abolitionism, temperance, education. But here too the religious faith was integrally related to its ethical and populist character—and, as Gordon Wood has shown, to its capitalist ethos, which made self-discipline a corollary of self-interest.[17] So too, the Third Great Awakening toward the end of the nineteenth century; very different from its predecessors, it was modernist in its theology and radical in its social views, preaching a social gospel that was critical of big business and supportive of labor unions, social reforms, and progressive causes. In each case, the revival spawned a host of sects that outnumbered the older churches by far, in both clerics and laity; even some of the smaller denominations were considerably larger than the Episcopal or Presbyterian churches. And the revivals themselves were constantly being reinvigorated by new preachers and ministers who infused their religious zeal with an entrepreneurial, populist spirit. One might say that they were trading in the free market of religion. The historian Nathan Hatch sees this spirit persisting to the present day: "Religious populism has been a residual agent of change in America over the last two centuries, an inhibitor of genteel tradition and a recurring source of new religious movements."[18]

The current revival, which has been called the Fourth Great Awakening, originated in the 1960s and continues to this day. The label reminds us that this is not a new (for many, a frighteningly new) phenomenon that we are witnessing but a familiar one. Yet it is even more diverse, theologically and socially, than the earlier ones. The movement as a whole—about 60 million people in 1988, the historian Robert Fogel estimates, or about a third of the adult population—is dominated by the fundamentalist, pentecostal, and charismatic Protestant denominations (generally lumped together under the label "evangelical"); but it also includes as many as 20 million members of the mainline

Protestant churches, 6 million "born again" Catholics, and almost 5 million Mormons.[19] These estimates vary widely, depending upon the definition of the terms. In a survey conducted in 1996, evangelicals were found to constitute one-fourth to one-fifth of the population;[20] in others, based upon more rigorous theological criteria, one-sixth to one-tenth.[21] Perhaps more significant is the number of people who describe themselves as "born again" or "evangelical"—almost half of the respondents in one poll in 1998.[22]

However defined, evangelicalism should not be confused with the "religious right," as it has been called—the conservative activist movement that has emerged so prominently in the political arena.* In one survey, only one-third of the evangelicals identify with the religious right;[24] in another, only one-fifth do.[25] Evangelicals are more varied, not only theologically and denominationally but also politically, than the popular image would have it. Not all are fundamentalist, or fundamentalist to the same degree. And not all are conservative, or conservative to the same degree. Whereas most adherents of the religious right are Republicans, almost half of the evangelicals who are not of the religious right are Democrats.[26] (In the election of 1998, it was reported that 40 percent of "religious conservatives" voted Democratic.[27])

Moreover, neither evangelicals nor the religious right conform to the familiar social stereotypes. They are not red-necked, retrograde philistines living in rural areas, fearful of change and

---

*Ralph Reed, the former director of the Christian Coalition, rejects the term "religious right" as historically inaccurate (it properly belongs, he says, only to the movement that arose in the New Right in the late 1970s), and as pejorative, connoting an extremist political agenda. No one, he points out, refers to the National Council of Churches as the "religious left."[23] The point is well taken, but because the "religious right" is often used in polls and commentaries, the term is now unavoidable.

modernity, anxious about their jobs and future. The evangelicals are, in fact, more highly educated than those calling themselves either religious liberals or secularists, and only slightly less likely to have had a graduate education than mainline Protestants. In other respects—employment, income, urban residence—they fit the pattern of the population at large.[28] The religious right differs even more from the stereotype. It consists of more women than men; almost half are between the ages of thirty-five and forty-nine; almost half live in the South; and in income, education, and social status they outrank both evangelicals in general and the population at large.[29]

All, however—evangelicals and the religious right—feel alienated from a culture that they see as inimical to both their religious and their cultural values. Stephen Carter tells the story of two black evangelical women who moved from liberal political groups to conservative ones for no other reason than the feeling that the liberals did not respect their religiosity. "They preferred a place," Carter comments, "that honored their faith and disdained their politics over a place that honored their politics and disdained their faith."[30]

The social issues central to this latest Great Awakening—abortion, prayer in the schools, sexual promiscuity—are very different from those animating the earlier ones, but they generate the same kind of passion. They also utilize much the same modes of preaching and sermonizing. Today's radio and television gospel meetings—there are now over 250 religious TV stations, compared with nine twenty-five years ago[31]—may be seen as a technologically updated version of Whitefield's preaching tours, which were also well publicized and organized and attracted huge congregations. (Whitefield has been called the "father of mass evangelism."[32])

Like Tocqueville, European visitors to the United States today may well be struck by the "religious atmosphere of the country," which is in striking contrast to the situation in their own countries.* In the United States, which has had no *ancien régime* to overcome and no tradition of anticlericalism, religion from the beginning has been the ally, rather than the enemy, of liberty. A multiplicity of sects and denominations, some of which are little more than "voluntary associations" freely entered into and departed from, is obviously more congenial to an individualistic culture than the firmly structured, hierarchical, often state-established European churches. For whatever reason, there is no doubt that Americans tend to be more religious than their European counterparts. In one survey (in 1993), 43 percent in the United States said they attended church at least weekly; in Britain 14 percent; in France 12 percent; in Sweden 4 percent. In the United States, 49 percent said that religion is very important in their lives (today that figure is 58 percent); in Britain 17 percent, in France 10 percent, in Sweden 8 percent.[36] The French press was startled in 1997 by the million or so young people who flooded Paris to hear the Pope celebrate Mass. But the fact is that only half of French youth today even call themselves Catholic (compared with almost 90 percent who did so

---

*It does not, however, surprise some non-European visitors. In a startling demonstration of ecumenicity, the President of Iran recently cited Tocqueville ("which I am sure most Americans have read") in praise of America as a civilization where "liberty found religion as a cradle for its growth and religion found protection of liberty as its divine calling."[33] Nor does it surprise visitors from Latin America or parts of East and Southeast Asia, which have experienced similar evangelical revivals. In Chile and Brazil, 15 percent to 20 percent of the population are now Protestant, and of these, the overwhelming majority are Pentecostals.[34] A Mexican sociologist explains why evangelicalism is especially attractive to the poor: "Evangelicals practice new ethics, another way of living. Usually the women are the first to convert. They see in the new religion a way to provide their families a better life. Evangelicals don't drink, a fact which makes an immediate difference in their lives because in many poor families, alcohol impacts their financial situation."[35]

three decades ago), and fewer than half of these actually practice their faith.[37]

Shortly after the papal visit in France, Václav Havel, President of the Czech Republic, addressed an international conference in Prague. Six years earlier he had deplored the moral condition of his country after its liberation from Communism.* He now took the occasion to lament the fact that the first global civilization is also "the first atheistic civilization in the history of humankind"—a surprising complaint from someone identified with an intellectual and literary elite not noted for its religiosity.

> Could not the whole nature of the current civilization, with its shortsightedness, with its proud emphasis on the human individual as the crown of all creation—and its master—and with its boundless trust in humanity's ability to embrace the Universe by rational cognition, could it not all be only the natural manifestation of a phenomenon which, in simple terms, amounts to a loss of God? Or more specifically: the loss of respect for the order of existence of which we are not the creators but mere components. Could it not be that the issue is a crisis of respect for the moral order extended to us from above, or simply a crisis of respect for any kind of authority higher than our own earthly being, with its material and thoroughly ephemeral earthly interests?[38]

The United States would seem to be notably exempt from the "global atheism" that so disturbs Havel. American sociologists speak of "the churching of America" as one of the most conspicuous aspects of American "exceptionalism."[39] A staggering 96 percent of Americans profess to believe in God or a

*See p. 43.

"universal spirit," and 90 percent in heaven. (In good American fashion, only 65 percent believe in the devil and 73 percent in hell.) 67 percent identify themselves as members of a church; 60 percent say they attend church at least once a month; 90 percent say that they pray at least once a week and 75 percent pray daily.[40] With only small variations, these findings hold for the better-educated as well as the less-educated, for the rich and the poor. (Those earning more than $75,000 a year are more likely to have attended religious services in the previous week than those earning less than $15,000.[41]) It may well be that people are reporting what they think they ought to be doing rather than what they actually do.[42] But this too is significant, reflecting values that are believed in even though they may not be observed in practice.*

Other statistics demonstrate the personal and social benefits associated with religious affiliation and observance. The practice of religion has a high correlation with family stability, communal activity, and charitable contributions; and a low correlation with suicide, depression, drug addiction, alcoholism, and crime. Black Protestants and white Catholics with similarly high church attendance have similarly low divorce rates. Those who seldom or never attend church have seven times the cohabitation rate of those who do. (This spills over into the following generation; children whose mothers frequently attend services are half as likely to cohabit as adults than those whose mothers are not church-goers.) Not "safe sex" but the regular practice of religion is one of the most important factors in preventing out-of-wedlock births. Religion has even been shown to be conducive to physical well-being. Regular church attendance is

---

*According to one survey in 1998, 58 percent believe the Bible to be "totally accurate in all it teaches"; 38 percent say they read the Bible during a typical week (outside of church); 22 percent claim to have read the entire Bible—and 12 percent say that the name of Noah's wife was Joan of Arc![43]

correlated with a stronger immune system and lower mortality rates from heart, liver, and lung diseases.[44]

These comforting statistics about religion would seem to be at odds with the discomforting ones about our social and moral condition. If religion is so important in the United States and if it seems to have such positive effects, why do so many people believe the country to be in a state of moral decline? Why are Americans, no less than Europeans, experiencing the "crisis of respect for the moral order" that Havel attributes to the "loss of God"?

The anomaly may be partly accounted for historically. Although the United States is far more religious than most European countries, it is also less religious than it once was. Here, as in so many other respects, the decisive changes occurred in the 1960s. At just the time that the rates of divorce, illegitimacy, crime, and drug addiction were rising, so the rates of church membership, attendance, prayer, and religious observances were declining—in the mainline churches, at any rate. (It was in reaction to both the mainline churches and the secular counterculture that the evangelical revival started about the same time.) It is striking, especially compared with other countries, that 58 percent of Americans today say that religion is very important in their lives, but less striking compared with the 75 percent who thought it very important in 1952; or that 66 percent today say that "religion can answer all or most of today's problems," compared with 82 percent in 1957.[45]

More significant is the varied and changing character of the churches, so that religious membership and attendance or even expressions of religiosity are no longer reliable indicators of moral and cultural dispositions. Tocqueville, living in a less secular, less diverse age, could assume that "each sect worships God in its own fashion, but all preach the same morality in the name of God."[46] That is no longer the case. The churches do not preach the same morality. Certainly, many of them do not preach anything like the morality that Tocqueville would have expected of them.

There has been much talk about the revival of religion on college campuses. But a good deal of that religion ("spirituality," as it is more popularly known) is eclectic and syncretic—New Age sects that have as little to do with traditional morality as with traditional religion. A researcher asked a college graduate what her religious preference was. "Methodist, Taoist, Native American, Quaker, Russian Orthodox, and Jew," she replied. This meant, she explained, that she "works for world peace, practices yoga and meditation, attends a Methodist church, regularly participates in American Indian ceremonies, and shares a group house with others who combine various spiritual practices." Traditional scholars describe this as "cafeteria-style" or "supermarket" spirituality. Others, better disposed to it, prefer the more dignified term "trans-religiosity." (Some of those who are actually engaged in this kind of ecumenicism are less reverent. Jews who practice Buddhist meditation refer to themselves as "Jewboos.")[47] And it is not only on campuses that this mode of spirituality thrives. Bookstores feature such best-selling books as *The Celestine Prophecy; The Ecstatic Journey: The Transforming Power of Mystical Experience; Kything: The Art of Spiritual Presence;* and, on a more mundane level, *Chicken Soup for the Teenage Soul.*

In addition to New Age faiths, non-Western religions are assuming a greater prominence. There are now about as many Muslims in the United States as Presbyterians. And the Muslims themselves are a heterogeneous group; less than one-third come from South Asia, one-quarter are African-American, and one-fifth are Arabs. (Contrary to the general impression, only one-third of Arab Americans are Muslim; the rest are Christian.)[48] This religious diversity, of the home-grown as well as immigrant variety, has as its corollary a considerable degree of moral and cultural diversity.

If New Age religions are not paragons of traditional morality, neither are the mainline churches. George Gallup, who has done extensive polling on the subject, speaks of "an ethics gap" between "the way we think of ourselves and the way we actually are"—between, in effect, religious faith and moral practices.[49] The sociologist James Davison Hunter dates this gap to the late 1950s and early '60s, when liberal Protestant theology was being redefined in "secular, humanistic terms," accommodating itself to the "worldview and 'life-styles' of modernity."[50] This process of accommodation has since gone on apace, so that today many mainline churches offer little or no resistance to the prevailing culture. On the contrary, some are very much part of it, priding themselves on being cosmopolitan and sophisticated, undogmatic and uncensorious. Thus they carefully avoid, in their sermons and public declarations, the old language of morality—"sin," "shame," "evil"—preferring the new language of sociability—"inappropriate," "unseemly," "improper."

This "ethics gap," or "great divide," as one scholar calls it, cuts through all religions and denominations.[51] Southern and Northern Baptists differ sharply not only on such subjects as the ordination of women and homosexuals but on cultural and moral values in general; and among Southern Baptists themselves the disagreements are serious enough to have very nearly caused a schism in the 1980s.* In 1998, the United Methodist

*The declaration, approved by the Southern Baptist Convention in June 1998, that wives should "submit" to their husbands (in accordance with the Epistle of Paul) was greeted with outrage, not only by the secular press but by those Southern Baptists who had come a long way from this literal reading of the gospels. The public had to be reminded that the Southern Baptists include not only some of the most prominent conservative politicians (former Speaker of the House Newt Gingrich, Majority Leader of the Senate Trent Lott, and Senator Strom Thurmond), but also some of the most liberal ones (President Clinton, Vice President Gore, former President Carter,

Church (the next-largest Protestant church after the Southern Baptists) confronted the prospect of secession over such issues as sexual morality and religious authority. All the churches (including Judaism) have been rent by disputes over gay marriages, with some ministers (and rabbis) performing such marriages privately and discreetly even though their denominations officially ban them.

Some Reform Jews regard marriage with an Orthodox Jew almost as a species of intermarriage, and would prefer their child to marry a non-Jew who shares their values rather than an Orthodox Jew who does not. Protestants allied with the National Council of Churches have not much more in common with those in the Christian Coalition than with nonbelievers; indeed, they may be better disposed to the latter because they do not contaminate the well of religion. Even evangelicals are divided between those practicing a "classical" spirituality derived from earlier Protestant and Puritan traditions, and those partial to a "postmodern" or "existential" spirituality, which is therapeutic and individualistic.[52] Catholics are also more diverse than might be supposed. "Cafeteria Catholics," as they are derogatorily called, observe only those teachings of the church that they find congenial. Four-fifths of all Catholics believe that birth control is "entirely up to the individual," and two-thirds that "one can be a good Catholic without going to Mass." Among those who call themselves "Modernists," little more than a third are opposed to abortion.[53]

If there are fractious divisions within the churches, there are also fraternal relations among them. In his important work *Culture Wars: The Struggle to Define America*, James Davison Hunter analyzes the "pragmatic alliances being formed across faith tradi-

House Minority Leader Richard Gephardt). The latter group can take comfort in the fact that this amendment to the "Faith and Message" credo of the Southern Baptists is not binding on its members, any more than the credo itself is.

tions," with cultural conservatives in all denominations allied against progressivists.[54] Other scholars speak of a shift from "ethnocultural" to "ideological" coalitions, resulting in "cross-tradition alliances" of liberals against conservatives.[55] The evangelicals, one historian points out, have been especially effective in creating a "transdenominational community" by the skillful use of radio, television, books, journals, and schools.[56]

These interfaith alliances make for strange bedfellows. Orthodox Jews sometimes discover that they have more in common with Protestant fundamentalists and Catholic traditionalists on such subjects as school vouchers, gay marriage, or sex education in the schools than with their brethren in the Reform or even Conservative denominations. A bill to put religious groups on an equal footing with the nonreligious in channeling government aid to the needy has the enthusiastic support of both evangelical Protestants and Orthodox Jews and the equally vociferous opposition of liberal Protestants and Reform Jews. The Christian Coalition has spawned a Catholic Alliance committed to the same social and moral values. And in spite of the traditional anti-Catholic bias among evangelicals, the leaders of both groups issued a manifesto, "Evangelicals and Catholics Together," asserting their common mission.[57] It is not unusual to find, at a religious conference, an Orthodox rabbi, a Catholic priest, and a black Baptist preacher sharing the head table with evangelicals.

The religious revival, then, is not only a religious revival. It is also a cultural and moral revival—and a communal one as well; like the Wesleyan movement, it provides a sense of community in a society that often appears to be anonymous and impersonal. This is not to deny or belittle the religious impulse in the movement, only to appreciate its ethical and social character. Christianity, one evangelical historian writes, has always looked upon "faith and morals as two sides of the same coin."[58] This is especially true in periods of social unrest, which is perhaps why the recent revival has bypassed the mainline churches.

While the Episcopalians, for example, have declined by one-quarter since 1960, the membership of the Pentecostal churches has increased fivefold.[59]

If the religious revival would bewilder a visiting European, it is no less bewildering to those Americans who have no strong religious convictions and are fearful of the intrusion, as they see it, of religion in public life. To some people, the very word "religion" conjures up the dreaded image of the religious right. In his aptly titled *The Culture of Disbelief,* Stephen Carter explains that in our present secular culture, citizens are told, in effect, that "it is fine to be religious in private, but there is something askew when those private beliefs become the basis for public action."[60] This argument, it has been pointed out, was not heard when the Reverend Martin Luther King led the movement for civil liberties, or when Protestant ministers denounced the Vietnam War, or when Catholic bishops called for a nuclear freeze, or when evangelicals rallied to the support of "born-again" Jimmy Carter. If religious conservatives are now accused of intruding improperly in political affairs, their defenders claim, it is not so much because they are religious as because they are conservative—because they do not subscribe to the conventional liberal positions on social or cultural issues.

The suspicion of the religious movement is especially conspicuous among journalists, who are generally liberal in politics and secular in belief. In 1993 a front-page story in the *Washington Post* described the "Gospel lobby" as "poor, uneducated, and easy to command."[61] Protests from readers obliged the *Post* to retract that statement. But much of the media continued to report upon religious events *de haut en bas*, as if describing the antics of some barbarian tribe. It was not until four years later, with the mass meeting of "Promise Keepers" in Washington—half-a-million men meeting for a day of prayer and atonement, pledging themselves to Christian observance, marital fidelity, and familial responsibility—that some journalists began to recognize that these were not the impoverished, benighted souls they were assumed to be. (Surveys of the Promise Keepers show them to be predominantly middle-class, with a disproportionate number of well-paid, well-educated professionals.)[62]*

The revival is also disconcerting to those academics who share the French Enlightenment view that religion is premodern and therefore obsolete. Peter Berger and other sociologists have long since refuted the idea that modernization necessarily implies secularization.[64] But intellectual habits die hard in the academy and that theory has persisted, perhaps because it is congenial to the secular disposition of most professors. It is interesting that the race/class/gender trinity so prominent in universities conspicuously omits religion. Nor does religion play much part in that other fashionable theme, multiculturalism, although it obviously has a crucial role in the formation of ethnic cultures.

Even in discussions of civil society, religion is often mentioned only in passing, the churches making a token appearance as one of the many "voluntary associations" of civil society. In one book, religion is missing from the "infrastructure" of morality that is said to be the basis of the community.[65] In others, it is dismissed on the grounds that it is "no longer the source of moral authority it once was,"[66] or that it is "unlikely to sustain us in the morality required of Progress."[67] In yet another, it makes an appearance only in the context of "religious liberty"

---

*This media hostility is not shared by most Americans. About three-quarters of the public say they regard the religious right as patriotic, well-meaning people of character and conviction who are concerned about the family and morality. And a large majority reject such characterizations of them as "backward," "low in education," "out of touch with reality," or "mean-spirited." Asked what general impression the term "Christian Right" evoked, 58 percent indicated positive feelings, 23 percent neutral, and only 19 percent negative.[63]

and in derogatory remarks about the religious right.[68] In still another, the single reference to religion in the index reads: "Religion: as therapy."[69]

The indifference or hostility to religion on the part of many intellectuals and academics has prompted two historians, both avowedly secular and liberal, to protest that such an attitude does justice neither to the reality of American life nor to their own cause. Writing in the left-wing *Nation*, Michael Kazin recalls a quotation in the *New York Times* from Katha Pollitt, a prominent feminist and columnist for the *Nation*, describing religion as "a farrago of authoritarian nonsense, misogyny and humble pie, the eternal enemy of human happiness and freedom." This antipathy to religion, Kazin says, is "myopic and self-defeating," for it denies the strong sense of spirituality and morality characteristic of the Christian left as well as right, which could be harnessed in the service of such progressive causes as health care, homes for the poor, the environment, and the like.[70]

Similarly, Alan Brinkley, in *Liberalism and Its Discontents*, rebukes his fellow liberal, secular intellectuals for failing to recognize that not all Americans share their progressive, rationalistic ideals. The fundamentalist right, he suggests, is not the "irrational, rootless 'lunatic fringe' plagued by cultural and psychological maladjustments" that it has been made out to be. Indeed, "fundamentalists can be rational, stable, intelligent people with a worldview radically different from their [the liberals'] own." It is the duty of historians and liberals, Brinkley reminds them, to understand these conflicting world views and the "cultural chasms" they have created among Americans.[71]

A few decades ago, the concept of "civil religion" enjoyed a great appeal among academics who wanted to credit the idea of religion in the abstract without committing themselves to any particular religion. Like "civil society," the term "civil religion" has a long heritage, but was dormant until it burst out in the late

1960s and '70s. ("Civil religion" predated the vogue for civil society by a decade, and its decline coincided with the rising interest in civil society in the '80s.) Popularized by the sociologist Robert Bellah in 1975 in *The Broken Covenant,* civil religion was said to be the "transcendent reality" that provided the moral underpinning of the American republic, the "covenant" that validated the principles of liberty, equality, and justice which were the basic tenets of the American "faith." This original covenant, Bellah regretfully reported, had been broken in recent times because of an economic system that propagates "every one of the classic vices of mankind": materialism, commercialism, corruption, and vulgarity.[72] In a revised edition of *The Broken Covenant* in 1992, Bellah retreated somewhat from this position. Describing the book as a "jeremiad," he professed to be dissatisfied with the concept of civil religion—not, he said, because it was inaccurate but because it was so mired down in definitional controversies that the substantive issue had been lost.[73]

If, as critics have argued, this idea of civil religion describes neither the founding nor the present condition of the United States, it is also a distortion of what Rousseau had in mind when he coined the term. (He introduced it belatedly, in a chapter appended to the *Social Contract* after the first draft had been completed.) Unlike Bellah, who made civil religion coexistent with Christianity, Rousseau intended it as an alternative to that "tyrannical" religion. Where Christianity, he said, "preaches only servitude and dependence," civil religion celebrates the virtues of a republic. Its dogmas are those "social sentiments without which a man cannot be a good citizen or a faithful subject": the belief in tolerance, in the social contract, in a beneficent deity, and in a hereafter that would bring happiness for the just and punishment for the wicked. Civil religion thus gives a divine sanction to the law and public service, providing a country with "its gods, its own tutelary patrons . . . its dogmas, its rites, and its external cult prescribed by law."[74]

It was just such a "cult" that Robespierre (who eulogized Rousseau as the "precursor" of the French Revolution and the "preceptor of the human race"[75]) adopted as the official religion of the "Republic of Virtue." The Cult of the Supreme Being, inaugurated on June 8, 1794, at an elaborate festival presided over by Robespierre, decreed nature its "priest" and the universe its "temple," prescribed festivals commemorating the glorious events of the Revolution, and created a Revolutionary calendar consisting of renamed months of equal length and "weeks" of ten days, each assigned a specific "virtue" or "blessing"—patriotism, friendship, love, conjugal fidelity, filial piety, the hatred of tyrants and traitors. Two days after that magnificent ceremony, the National Convention passed another measure, also introduced by Robespierre, known (in accordance with the new Revolutionary calendar) as the Law of the 22d Prairial. It was this act that officially instituted the Terror.

The Cult of the Supreme Being is surely not what the modern enthusiasts of civil religion had in mind when they took up that idea.* Nor would most of them have approved of the religious revival that was beginning to take place in the United States at just the time that they were rediscovering civil religion. A cover story by *Newsweek* in 1976 declared that year, the bicentenary of the American Revolution, to be the "Year of the Evangelical."[78] This evangelicalism, theologically orthodox and sometimes fundamentalist, bore no resemblance to anything like a civil religion. *Newsweek* cited a Gallup poll in

---

*Other sources cited for the modern idea of civil religion (although not the term itself) are Tocqueville, who, according to one interpretation, amalgamated American character with American Christianity to produce something like a civil religion[76]; or Emile Durkheim, who identified all religions (not only Christianity) with "the collective sentiments and the collective ideas which make its [society's] unity and its personality." "The idea of society," Durkheim pronounced, "is the soul of religion."[77]

which one-third of Americans described themselves as "born again" and almost half of all Protestants said that the Bible should be taken literally. If civil religion is religion for the non-religious, as one critic has said,[79] the evangelical revival is decidedly religion for the religious.

Recently, the revival has taken on a new task—not only the religious and spiritual revitalization of society, but also the moral and social rehabilitation of the "underclass." Like civil society and the polity, religion has been engaged in the enterprise of seeking "democratic remedies for the diseases of democratic societies"—in this case, "faith-based" remedies.

Members of churches and religious groups have always been disproportionately active in volunteer and charitable enterprises. But only in the past decade or so have there been sophisticated, sustained efforts by ministers and local churches to supplement or even replace public, secular social programs by private, religious ones. And for the first time these are receiving the respectful attention of social scientists, who find that they often succeed in doing, if only on a small scale, what government programs have notably failed to do. It is a sign of the times that in 1999 the liberal *Brookings Review* devoted an entire issue to this subject under the title "What's God to Do with the American Experiment?"

The criminologist John DiIulio, who has been personally involved in these efforts and has set up a research organization for this purpose, has eloquently described the work of inner-city ministers who have labored, often anonymously and against great odds, to redeem the youth in their crime-ridden, drug-infested communities. He quotes a conversation between the Rev. Eugene F. Rivers, the pentecostal minister of the Azusa Christian Community Church in Boston—himself a former gang member—and the local drug dealer:

"Man [the Minister asks the dealer], why did we lose you? Why are we losing other kids now?" He stares us in the eye and says, "I'm there, you're not. When the kids go to school, I'm there, you're not. When the boy goes for a loaf of bread or wants a pair of sneakers or just somebody older to talk to or feel safe and strong around, I'm there, you're not. I'm there, you're not; I win, you lose."[80]

With the cooperation of other religious leaders and lay volunteers, Rivers tries to ensure that they are "there" by policing local gangs, monitoring juvenile probation, and being available, on a daily and personal basis, to at-risk youths. The result has been a dramatic reduction of juvenile crime in Boston. In a single year, 1995–96, the murder rate in Boston dropped by almost 40 percent; since then there has been exactly one murder of a juvenile in Boston, compared with seventy in Washington, D.C., and almost that number in Baltimore.[81] Heartened by these results, a group of clergymen has created a national organization with the aim of mobilizing a thousand inner-city churches in forty of the most blighted areas of the nation's largest cities.

Another faith-based program is the Restorative Justice movement directed to non-violent criminals, who, instead of being jailed, confront their victims personally and pledge restitution and community service. Unlike the old mode of rehabilitation, which tries to reform criminals by psychological therapy and vocational training, this requires a recognition on the part of offenders that they have violated a moral law and must make moral as well as material atonement. One such experiment in western New York State (ironically, ten miles north of Attica prison) has resulted in substantial sums paid to victims, hundreds of thousands of hours of community service, and, perhaps more significantly, a recidivism rate less than half that of criminals sentenced to prison or probation.[82]

Still another, the Prison Fellowship initiated by Charles Colson (the Watergate felon and an evangelical convert), operates within prisons to "create a climate where spiritual and moral rebirth can take place, where inmates can restore and develop their relationship with God, their families, and their communities."[83] After their release from jail, the Fellowship keeps in touch with them, trying to repair their family life and putting them in contact with neighborhood churches. "Bible-based and Christ-centered," this program is explicitly sectarian; non-Christians can attend the meetings, but the goal is Christian conversion. It has no expectation of redeeming all those who come under its sway, but it may be responsible for the rehabilitation of a significant number. In one survey, 14 percent of those who participated regularly in Prison Fellowship were rearrested within a year of their release, compared with 41 percent of those who did not attend.[84]

There are by now a multitude of faith-based programs sponsored by local religious groups and churches, largely or entirely staffed by volunteers, catering to alcoholics and drug addicts, abandoned and abused children, school dropouts, the sick and incapacitated, immigrants, the homeless, pregnant teen-agers, inner-city fatherless boys, and poor single mothers. Among the most ambitious programs are those adopted in the wake of the welfare reform act. A provision of the act, passed with bipartisan support, gives local communities the "charitable choice" of assigning public welfare services to faith-based agencies. As a result, some states and cities now "contract out" welfare families to churches and religious groups, which provide not only financial and material assistance but counseling and spiritual and moral guidance.

What these grass-roots programs have in common, apart from their religious and moral emphasis, is the personal relationship between the giver and the recipient of aid. Robert Woodson, who has been in the forefront of this movement, insists upon the "zip-code test"; those who serve the poor should reside in the same neighborhood as those they are serving.[85] Observers testify to the fact that these programs succeed, and do so where secular, public agencies often fail, only to the extent to which they retain their distinctive character. But they also acknowledge the great difficulties they confront. DiIulio concludes that "not even an army of well-led, well-supported churches and faith-based programs could save the nation's most severely at risk children, revitalize blighted neighborhoods, and resurrect the civil society of inner-city America without the active human and financial support of suburban churches, secular civil institutions, profit-making corporations, and, last but not least, government at all levels."[86]

That "last but not least" is the snag. Almost everyone involved in these enterprises (including DiIulio) agrees that government funding is perilous, often undermining the spiritual and ethical principles that make these projects effective. Indeed, even programs not subsidized by the government are hindered by official regulations about safety and sanitary conditions, wages and professional credentials, and legal and bureaucratic requirements that are unrealistic and economically prohibitive.* Government funding exacerbates these problems, for it almost invariably leads to a dilution or elimination of both the moral and the religious character of the programs. It also makes it difficult for them to impose conditions on those they are assisting—"tough-love" requirements of work, regular attendance at classes or religious

---

*Woodson gives a typical example. Victory Fellowship, a successful substance-abuse program that receives no government funds, has among its most effective employees recovered addicts. The government threatens to shut it down because the staff does not hold the academic degrees necessary for certification. The Fellowship is also prohibited from taking in young people living on the street who come to it for safe haven—because they are minors.[87]

services, abstention from alcohol and drugs. Thus it subverts their very purpose, which is the development of a sense of individual responsibility and moral accountability. The director of a shelter for the homeless describes the fatal flaws of government subsidies: "an exaggerated emphasis on 'entitlements' and 'rights,' a one-size-fits-all cookie-cutter mentality, a deadening secularization that freezes out religious wisdom and motivation, and a hopelessly gargantuan scale that prevents human trust and connectedness from ever growing up between aid-giver and aid recipient."[88]

Those who have concluded, however reluctantly, that faith-based programs require some government support have first to overcome the legal objection that this violates the separation of church and state—an argument challenged by constitutional scholars like Stephen Carter[89]—and then to devise ways of minimizing the intrusiveness of the government. The mayor of Indianapolis proposes taking as the first rule for such private/public enterprises a variation on the Hippocratic Oath: "Government must do no harm to these community building organizations."[90]

These "value-shaping organizations" (as the Indianapolis program puts it) have been commended as the most promising means of coping with the "depth of psychic and moral decay" in the inner city, described so graphically by Rivers.[91] If this sounds like the language of the religious right, it should be said that Rivers, like many of his associates, is very much of the left. In fact, the distinction between right and left is irrelevant in this context. What is relevant is the distinction between private religious and moral initiatives of this kind and the secular agencies of the government. The crucial question is whether the former can supplant or significantly supplement the latter—whether faith-based organizations can cope not only with the "depth of psychic and moral decay," but also with the extent of that decay. Those who do not think that private resources are sufficient have the task of establishing a viable working relationship between the private and the public, the religious and the secular, determining the parameters, functions, and responsibilities of each.

Two-and-a-half centuries after Diderot's famous pronouncement "Let us strangle the last king with the entrails of the last priest," religion is alive and well, and not only in the fundamentalist Near East but in the most modern of Western countries. This is what disturbs many American liberals and secularists. They tend to be tolerant of progressive, mainline churches and of syncretic New Age spirituality. But they feel threatened by orthodox or fundamentalist religions that they see as not only overly doctrinaire in faith but also presumptuous in thinking that faith has any bearing on morality, let alone any exclusive claim to moral authority. They are repelled by the self-righteousness, self-aggrandizement, and self-enrichment of some preachers, all the more so in the light of recent sordid and well-publicized scandals, sexual and financial. Many are also offended by what they take to be an intolerance of those of other faiths (or of little faith), and an excessive harshness toward those of other "lifestyles"—homosexuals, most notably.

They also suspect that beneath the religious agenda of evangelicalism is a political, partisan one, that it is the tool of the Republican Party and of the social-conservative faction within the party. "The Religious Right," the headline of one article reads, "Is About Politics, not Faith."[92] Their fears are not allayed by repeated demonstrations of the fact that the political process tends to be resistant to any designs the religious right might have upon it, and that the Republican Party is still dominated by a largely secular business community and by pragmatic, nonideological politicians.

More ominous, for liberals and secularists, is what they take to be the theocratic aspirations of evangelicals, an attempt to breach the wall separating church and state and impose sectarian beliefs and practices upon the country at large; the image is of an Islamic-like orthodoxy enforced by a monolithic state church. The language of some evangelicals gives credence to such suspicions; they are apt to refer casually to "Christian America." And there are undoubtedly some among them who do cherish ambitious hopes for the "Christianization" of the country. But this kind of zealotry (bigotry, some would say) is repudiated by most leaders of the religious right today (including some who have used such expressions in the past) and is not typical of the evangelical movement as a whole.

The argument about the separation of church and state cuts both ways. If secularists are concerned about the improper infusion of religion into the affairs of state, evangelicals worry that secularism itself is being made the official credo of the nation, the new civil religion. Instead of the old doctrine of the separation of church and *state*, evangelicals see the rise of a new doctrine of the separation of church and *society*, which would secularize society as well as the state. It is secularists, they say, who impinge on the autonomy of religion by protesting against beliefs or actions that involve the churches alone—the decision, for example, of some churches not to admit women to the clergy, or the statement by the Southern Baptists asserting the wife's subordination to her husband—as if such actions are a threat to American women in general, an attempt to relegate them all to an inferior status. Stephen Carter, an Episcopalian who is not sympathetic to religious fundamentalism, explains why such secularist objections are misplaced.

> Criticisms of this kind miss the point of the religions as alternative sources of meaning for their adherents: the truth is that outsiders have no standpoint from which to judge what counts as a "superior" or "inferior" position or, indeed, whether the words have any meaning within the

faith community. This is what it means to treat the religions as autonomous communities of resistance and as independent sources of meaning.[93]

In fact, it is precisely the autonomy and plurality of these religions that should be reassuring to liberals and secularists. "Evangelicalism," "fundamentalism," "the religious revival," and "the religious right" are daunting as singular nouns. But the reality is pluralistic. These collective terms embrace a multiplicity of groups, each with its own organizational identity, its own leaders, its own credo, and its own agenda—its own "subculture," as one historian puts it.[94] "Fundamentalism," Father Richard Neuhaus has said, "is magnificently fissiparous."[95]*

What these religious groups have in common is not a specific theological creed, let alone a theocratic agenda, but a shared religious sensibility and moral concern. So far from seeking to create a big-brother government in their own image, still less a state-supported church, they want a less intrusive government, one that will not impinge upon the domain of family or church. They are more comfortable with local governments than with the federal government (religious Republicans are three times more opposed to spending by Washington than secular Republicans, but twice as supportive of spending by localities[98]), and more comfortable still with civil society as the agent for moral and social reformation.

Liberals and secularists might also take consolation in the fact that the most activist of the groups spawned by the revival

---

*Recounting the recent history of turmoil in the Baptist Southern Convention, one Baptist theologian remarks: "Baptists have always been a fractious and fissiparous folk."[96] In that same fractious spirit, Bob Jones (founder of the fundamentalist Bob Jones University) denounces Jerry Falwell (of the Moral Majority) as "the most dangerous man in America so far as Biblical Christianity is concerned."[97]

tend to be short-lived. In the entrepreneurial spirit characteristic of so many American ventures, religious organizations rise and thrive for a time, only to subside and be succeeded by other organizations. This was the fate of the Moral Majority after only a decade of life, and there are already signs that both the Christian Coalition and the Promise Keepers are in financial straits. More recently, Paul Weyrich, the doyen of the religious right, has created a schism in the movement by suggesting that it withdraw from the political arena and pursue a separatist strategy.

While secularists complain of an increasingly articulate and active religious movement, religious groups feel beleaguered by a Supreme Court that has abandoned long-standing traditions and customs. Among the crucial events triggering the religious revival have been decisions banning prayers in public schools, legalizing abortion, and prohibiting the display of the Ten Commandments on school walls. In each case, the Court altered arrangements that had been in place for a century or more, sometimes since the founding of the Republic. And in each case it was not the religious party that was seeking a new and more privileged position for itself; it was the secular party that was the innovator. The sociologist Nathan Glazer describes the religious movement as being in a "defensive offensive" position. Abortion, he points out, became an issue not because the pro-life party wanted to strengthen restrictions or prohibitions, but because the pro-choice party abolished them (and abolished, too, the traditional jurisdiction of the states). Similarly, school prayers became a *cause célèbre* not because the religious wanted new, more sectarian prayers, but because they wanted to retain the old nondenominational ones.[99]

The Dissent of the Governed is the title Stephen Carter gives to his account of religious conservatives who feel (properly, in his opinion) that their moral values and religious traditions are being ignored or violated by an increasingly secular society.[100] He might have quoted Edmund Burke on the nature of that dissent. In his speech on "Conciliation with the Colonies," Burke explained that while the Americans derived their love of liberty from their mother country, it was enhanced by the special nature of their religion, a religion that agreed in nothing but "the communion of the spirit of liberty."

> The people are Protestants, and of that kind which is the most adverse to all implicit submission of mind and opinion. This is a persuasion not only favourable to liberty, but built upon it. . . . All protestantism, even the most cold and passive, is a sort of dissent. But the religion most prevalent in our northern colonies is a refinement on the principle of resistance: it is the dissidence of dissent, and the protestantism of the Protestant religion.[101]*

It is this "dissidence of dissent," evident in the plurality of sects, that so impressed Tocqueville when he visited the United States. And it was this that prompted his famous observation that religion was the warrant of liberty for Americans, "the first of their political institutions."

---

*In *Culture and Anarchy*, Matthew Arnold, defending the principle of a religious establishment, quoted, with great contempt, the slogan of one Nonconformist newspaper: "The Dissidence of Dissent and the Protestantism of the Protestant Religion."[102] One wonders whether Arnold, a great admirer of Burke, knew the provenance of that phrase.

CHAPTER VI
THE TWO CULTURES:
"AN ETHICS GAP"

The moral divide that Adam Smith saw in his society, indeed, in "every civilized society," was a class divide; it separated the rich and the poor, the "people of fashion" and the "common people." The divide we are confronting today cuts through class lines, as it also does through religious, racial, ethnic, political, and sexual lines.

Jean Jaurès, the French socialist and member of the Chamber of Deputies early in this century, is reputed to have said: "There is more in common between two parliamentarians one of whom is a socialist, than between two socialists one of whom is a parliamentarian." So, an American might now say, there is more in common between two church-going families one of which is working class, than between two working-class families only one of which is church-going; or between two two-parent families one of which is black, than between two black families only one of which has two parents. It is because their identity is defined primarily by moral and cultural values that many inner-city black parents send their children to Catholic schools, not because they themselves are Catholic (they often are not) but because they want their children to have a more rigorous education in a more disciplined environment than is available in the public schools. For the same reason, some nonobservant Jews send their children to Jewish day schools rather than public or even private secular schools.

The "pragmatic alliances" across religious lines, with cultural conservatives (or "traditionalists") in all faiths finding common cause against liberals (or "progressivists"), is paralleled by pragmatic alliances across political lines. It was the culture rather than economics that prompted many working-class Democrats to switch their lifelong allegiance and vote for Reagan in 1980. And it is cultural differences that are reflected in regional politics. One pollster speaks of the "bi-coastal liberalism" that unites the New England and Pacific states in their views of abortion, homosexuality, and religious faith, in contrast to the rest of the country.[1] Racial segregation is also giving way under the pressure of shared religious and moral concerns. Traditionally white Southern Baptist churches are opening their doors to blacks, and evangelicals are endorsing and even aggressively pursuing a policy of "racial reconciliation."[2]

The cultural divide helps explain the peculiar, almost schizoid nature of our present condition: the evidence of moral disarray on the one hand and of a religious-*cum*-moral revival on the other. This disjunction is apparent in small matters and large—in the fact, for example, that both gangsta rap and gospel rock are among today's fastest-growing forms of music; or that while raunchy talk shows are common on television, moralistic ones are on radio; or that while a good many people were tolerant of President Clinton's sexual infidelities, many others purchased enough copies of William Bennett's *Death of Outrage* (most of whom presumably share his outrage) to have kept it on the best-seller list for months.

The polarization is most conspicuous in such hotly disputed issues as abortion, gay marriage, school vouchers, and prayers in public schools. But it has larger ramifications, affecting beliefs, attitudes, values, and practices on a host of subjects ranging from private morality to public policy, from popular culture to high culture, from crime to education, welfare, and the family. In some respects, it is even more divisive than the class polarization that Karl Marx saw as the crucial fact of life under capitalism.

Having been spared the class revolution that Marx predicted, we have succumbed to the cultural revolution. What was, only a few decades ago, a subculture in American society has been assimilated into the dominant culture. For some time conservatives resisted acknowledging this, convinced that "the people," as distinct from "the elites," were still "sound," still devoted to traditional values, and that only superficially and intermittently were they (or more often their children) seduced by the blandishments of the counterculture. That confidence has eroded, as surely as the values themselves have. The old "bourgeois" ethos was never quite as "austere" as some might think, but it was considerably more so than the dominant ethos today. An "adversary culture" once confined to artists and artists-manqués— "bohemians," as they were called—has been democratized and popularized. (We no longer use the label "bohemian" because there is no longer any distinctive group that can claim it.) "Alternative lifestyles" that were frowned upon by polite society not so long ago are now not only tolerated but given equal status with traditional lifestyles. Manners and morals once taken for granted are now derided as puritanical and hypocritical.

Indeed, the very language of morality has been transformed, so that once honorific words are now pejorative. To pass moral judgments is to be "judgmental" and "moralistic"; to engage in moral discourse is to "preach" and "moralize"; to pronounce upon moral affairs is to wage a "moral crusade," or, worse, a "religious crusade." With the disparagement of the moral vocabulary comes a trivialization of morality itself. It is not on moral grounds that school counselors caution against promiscuity but on health grounds; "safe sex" means protected promiscuity. And when chastity is recommended, it is not as a moral virtue but as the safest form of safe sex, the only truly reliable safeguard against AIDS. "The core of the modern sexual code," Charles Krauthammer has said, "is disease prevention."[3] In the same spirit, smoking has replaced fornication as a major social vice, and neglecting to use seat belts is punishable while obscenity is not.

Like all cultures, the dominant culture today exhibits a wide spectrum of beliefs and practices. At one end is what sociologists refer to as the "elite culture." Statistics confirm what we all know, that the media and academia are consistently more permissive and progressive than the public at large. Thus only a quarter of the public but 90 percent in the media support the right of abortion without any qualifications.[4] Or more than three-quarters of the public but fewer than half in the media think that adultery is always wrong.[5] Or well over half of the public but only 5 percent of leading filmmakers attend church at least once a month.[6] The story of the professor who says that he cannot understand how President Reagan could have been elected, when he knows no one who voted for him, is not at all apocryphal; I have had that said to me in almost exactly those words on several occasions.*

The elite is only a small if a most visible and influential part of this culture. The bulk of it consists of people who are generally passive and acquiescent. Most lead lives that, in most respects, most of the time, conform to traditional ideals of morality and propriety. But they do so with no firm confidence in the principles underlying their behavior. Thus they are vulnerable to weaknesses and stresses in their own lives, and undermined by the example of their less conventional peers or those

---

*Professors of education are similarly more permissive than either parents or teachers. Only 37 percent think it important to maintain discipline in the classroom; 19 percent to stress spelling, grammar, and punctuation; 12 percent to expect students to be on time and polite.[7]

whom they might think of as their superiors. More important, they find it difficult to transmit their own principles and practices to their children. Even when they complain about the "moral decline" of the country (which they continue to do, in very large numbers), they offer little resistance to the manifestations of that decline. They believe in God, but they believe even more in the autonomy of the individual. They confess that they find it difficult to judge what is moral or immoral even for themselves, still more for others. Thus they habitually take refuge in such equivocations as "Who is to say what is right or wrong?" or "Personally, I disapprove of pornography [or promiscuity, or whatever], but that is only my own opinion."

Americans are often accused by Europeans of being "moralistic." In fact, the prevalent mode in America today is quite the opposite: a reluctance, even refusal, to pass moral judgments—to be, as is said, "judgmental." Europeans used to complain of the Americanization (the "coca-colaization") of European culture. They may be getting their revenge by witnessing the Europeanization (or de-moralization) of American culture.

Nearly all Americans profess to believe in "family values," but what they believe in is not necessarily the traditional family. One is not surprised to find sociologists redefining the family and renaming it the "postmodern family," including within it almost any combination or permutation of members; some dismiss the very idea of "family" (encapsulated in quotation marks) as having no objective meaning at all.[8] It is surprising, however, to find that almost three-quarters of the public now reject the traditional (and until recently legal) concept of family as people related by blood, marriage, or adoption, in favor of the expansive notion of "a group of people who love and care for each other."[9]

Most people have misgivings about "sexually active" teenagers, but they tend to be tolerant of sexually active college students and adults. 55–60 percent of the public think that premarital sexual relations are "acceptable" or "not wrong," and much the same number that out-of-wedlock births are acceptable.[10] And while more than 75 percent believe adultery to be "morally wrong," almost 70 percent say that they personally know men who have had such affairs and 35 percent do not "think less" of them for that. (The traditional double standard seems to have been reversed; 60 percent know women who have had affairs, and 40 percent do not think less of them for that.)[11]

For public figures, morality, like deviancy, is being defined down. In 1988, Gary Hart was forced out of the presidential campaign by a report of sexual philandering—not sexual harassment, but a single, consensual, extramarital relationship. (The most damning evidence against him was the photograph of a "model" amiably seated on his lap.) A decade later, after many more serious and salacious allegations, President Clinton enjoyed the highest approval ratings of his career. Although he was judged of singularly poor character, this was not seen as a disqualification for high office. The dichotomy, commentators say, is the result of a booming economy. But it also reflects a larger moral latitude accorded to public figures. Where once they were held to a higher moral standard than ordinary people—indeed, regarded as "role models"—now they are held to a lower standard. Power, we are told, is an aphrodisiac; politicians exude a sexuality they cannot control and others cannot resist.

As morality has been defined down for public figures, so it has been for the public as well. What the President is being accused of, many people are reported as saying, is what most men commonly do; it is not so much misconduct as normal masculine conduct. Thus the latitude allowed to the President has been extended to the public. By the same token, all "consensual sexual relations" are regarded as personal, private affairs, exempt from moral judgment. In the latter-day version of the Ten Commandments, "Thou shalt not commit adultery" has been replaced by "Thou shall not commit a judgment."

. . .

The reluctance to be judgmental pervades all aspects of life. In the university, it takes the form of postmodernism. In scholarly books and journals, "truth," "objectivity," "knowledge," even "reality," commonly appear ensconced within quotation marks, testifying to the ironic connotation of such quaint words. If these concepts are dubious, moral judgments are still more so. The language of "right" and "wrong," "virtue" and "vice," are made to seem as archaic as the language of "truth" and "objectivity," "knowledge" and "reality."

Until recently, even the most committed postmodernists have hesitated to "deconstruct" so horrifying a reality as the Holocaust or to be nonjudgmental about it. What some professors are now discovering is that the relativistic mode of thought has so successfully transmitted itself to students that they are prepared to do what their elders have prudently refrained from doing. In the *Chronicle of Higher Education*, Robert Simon, a professor of philosophy, reports that while none of his students denies the reality of the Holocaust, an increasing number do worse: they acknowledge the fact, even deplore it, but cannot bring themselves to condemn it morally. "Of course I dislike the Nazis," one student comments, "but who is to say they are morally wrong." They make similar observations about apartheid, slavery, and ethnic cleansing. To pass judgment, they fear, is to be a moral "absolutist," and having been taught that there are no absolutes, they now see any judgment as arbitrary, intolerant, and authoritarian.[12]*

---

*Simon's students are not unique. James Q. Wilson reports that some of his Harvard students were similarly reluctant to pass judgment on the perpetrators of the Holocaust. "It all depends on your perspective," one said. And another: "I'd just have to see these events through the eyes of the people affected by them."[13]

Another article in the same issue of the *Chronicle* recounts a similar experience by an instructor of creative writing. For more than twenty years Kay Haugaard had been reading with her class the famous story by Shirley Jackson, "The Lottery," about a small town where a woman is stoned to death by a crowd, including her husband and two children, as part of an annual sacrificial ritual to make the crops grow. Until recently, the story elicited from her students expressions of shock, horror, and unequivocal moral indignation. Lately, she has been receiving quite different reactions. One student tells her that the story is "neat" and that she "liked it," another that it is "all right" but not "that great." Yet another explains that the stoning seems to be like a religious ritual, in which case she cannot pass judgment on it or even decide whether the author approves or disapproves of it—this, Haugaard observes, from a student who objects passionately to killing whales and destroying rain forests. Another recalls a theory he had once read about cultures that require occasional bloodshed; "It almost seems a need," he coolly observes. An older student, a nurse, explains that she teaches a course at the hospital on multicultural understanding: "If it is part of a person's culture, we are taught not to judge, and if it has worked for them . . ." Not one student, in a class of twenty, spoke up in opposition to the moral obtuseness and cruelty portrayed in this gruesome tale.[14]

Other professors report upon students responding sympathetically to human sacrifice as practiced by the Aztecs or the scalping of enemies by Indians, while protesting against female circumcision among African tribes or experiments for medical purposes on rats. In the culture of academia, there are a few absolutes left, such as women's rights and animal rights; there are even a few vices, notably smoking and sexual harassment. With these exceptions, however, academia exhibits, in a more pronounced form, the relativism characteristic of the dominant culture—a relativism bordering on what Professor Simon calls "absolutophobia."

.   .   .

— There is, however, another culture (or set of loosely allied sub-cultures) that coexists somewhat uneasily with the dominant culture. This might be called the "dissident culture"—the culture not of the three-quarters of the public who redefine family to include "significant others," but of the one-quarter who abide by the traditional definition; not of the 55–60 percent who think that premarital sex is acceptable, but of the 40–45 percent who think it is not.[15] If the dominant culture is the heir of the counterculture, the dissident culture represents a counter-counterculture, a reaction against the increasingly prevalent and increasingly "looser" system of morals. The historian Nathan Hatch describes the resurgence of fundamentalism in the last few decades as a "populist crusade, a revolt of people who feel they are being disfranchised from the core institutions of American culture."[16] But it is not only fundamentalists who feel disfranchised; so, too, does a much larger and more varied sector of the population, including many people who are not notably religious but who do have strong moral concerns.

Like the dominant culture, the dissident culture exhibits a wide spectrum of beliefs and behavior, ranging from a rigid adherence to traditional values only occasionally violated in practice, to a more lenient set of values more often violated. But even the laxer representatives of this dissident culture tend to subscribe to a more "austere" moral code, and to do so more consciously, than their counterparts in the dominant culture. They do not think of sexual morality as a "personal matter" that can be "boxed off," as is now said, from the rest of life. Nor do they think of religion as a "private affair" that should not encroach upon the "public square." Nor are they apt to engage in such circumlocutions as "Who am I to say . . . ?" or "Personally . . . but . . ."

At one end of the spectrum of this dissident culture, paralleling the "elites" of the dominant culture, is the religious right, a hard core of determined and articulate activists. Although this group receives the most public attention, it is only a small part of this culture, for beyond it is a much larger and more varied group of evangelicals, as well as traditionalists in other churches —mainline Protestants, conservative Catholics, Mormons, and some Orthodox Jews. There is also a growing number of people who have no particular religious affiliation or disposition—may even be decidedly secular-minded—but do have strong moral convictions that put them at odds with the dominant culture.

Although this dissident culture is an important and often vocal presence in both society and the polity (neither political party can ignore it with impunity), it represents a minority of the population. Perhaps the most reliable quantitative estimate emerges from a study directed by two sociologists at the University of Virginia, James Davison Hunter and Carl Bowman, published in three volumes under the apt title *The State of Disunion*. Based on over 2,000 face-to-face interviews, each of an hour or more, conducted by the Gallup organization in 1996, the work surveys the "political culture," a concept that embraces moral and cultural as well as political attitudes. The study finds the nation divided into six groups: two "traditional" ones ("traditionalists" and "neo-traditionalists") together constituting 27 percent of the population; two "moderate" ones ("conventionalists" and "pragmatists"), 29 percent; and two "liberal" ones ("communitarians" and "permissivists"), 46 percent.[17]

As a minority, the traditionalist culture labors under the disadvantage of being perennially on the defensive. Its elite— gospel preachers, radio talk-show hosts, some prominent columnists, and organizational leaders—cannot begin to match, in numbers or influence, those who occupy the commanding heights of the dominant culture: professors presiding over the multitude of young people who attend their lectures, read their books, and have to pass their exams; journalists who determine what information, and what "spins" on that information, come to the public; television and movie producers who provide the images and values that shape the popular culture; cultural entrepreneurs who are ingenious in creating and marketing ever more sensational and provocative products. An occasional boycott by religious conservatives (of the Disney enterprises, for example) can hardly counteract the cumulative, pervasive effect of the dominant culture.

The "two cultures," needless to say, are neither monolithic nor static. Nor are they totally separate and distinct. They are not fixed, reified entities but loose categories or concepts representing a complex of values and beliefs which are shared, not entirely but in good measure, by "like-minded" people. But even like-minded people can and do differ. Some individuals are more permissive in respect to premarital sex, for example, than adultery, or feel more strongly about welfare dependency than sexual promiscuity, or are more troubled by violence and crime than obscenity and vulgarity. Yet in general, there is a common set of mind, a confluence of values and beliefs, that locates most people, most of the time, for most purposes, within one or the other culture.

It is also important to remember that the values and beliefs of individuals do not always correspond with their conduct. There is a powerful cultural lag that permits individuals to abide by social conventions while subscribing to a set of beliefs that countenances, or may even encourage, a quite different kind of behavior on the part of others (or of themselves, under certain conditions). It is this commonality of behavior that permits people of dissimilar values to live together civilly and amicably. Yet values do assert themselves—on public issues if not in private lives, and at times of crisis (such as the impeachment of a president) if not of tranquillity. It is then that the two cultures come to the fore, causing dissension in civil society and even in the political domain.

The dynamics between the cultures are complicated and unpredictable. As the dominant elites become more audacious in "pushing the envelope," as is said, they provoke a reaction on the part of many who otherwise acquiesce in the values of the dominant culture. Even a notably tolerant person might be dismayed by the new children's game on the Internet which is promoted as the goriest yet produced (invented, as if to compound the offense, by the creators of *Sesame Street*);[18] or by the video games and movies that so eerily prefigured the Littleton school massacre;[19] or by the play by an award-winning playwright featuring a homosexual Christ figure having sexual relations with his apostles;[20] or by the Distinguished Professor of English and Comparative Literature who flaunts her relations (heterosexual and homosexual) with her students as a higher form of scholarship and pedagogy;[21] or by the many other ways in which the popular and the high culture conspire together to deride and violate traditional conventions, values, and beliefs.

⬩ On the other hand, "pushing the envelope" may also have the contrary effect of inuring people to such excesses, so that they come to accept as normal and tolerable what would once have been shocking and repellent. Television provides an interesting case-study of this "defining deviancy down" phenomenon. The *New York Times*, hardly an organ of the religious right, has been reporting on the tendency of television shows to become more and more provocative even as the public becomes more and more complaisant. In July 1997 it described one highly acclaimed TV serial as "push[ing] the limits of network television" and "stretching the acceptable"—that is, setting new standards of violence, profanity, and prurience.[22] The following month it remarked on the frequent and graphic appearance of adultery and promiscuity on television, with the favorable portrayals of casual sex outnumbering the unfavorable by twenty to one.[23] In April 1998 it found TV stretching the "limits of taste" still further: "Like a child acting outrageously naughty to see how far he can push his parents, mainstream television this season is flaunting the most vulgar and explicit sex, language and behavior that it has ever sent into American homes." The *Times* was astonished that there was no public outcry, ratings continued to be high, advertisers were not discouraged, and parents were seemingly reconciled to such shows.[24] Two weeks later, it reported upon a new survey demonstrating that two-thirds of all prime-time network shows had scenes of violence, and nearly three-quarters of these scenes were accompanied by "no remorse, criticism or penalty."[25] A few months later it quoted the executives of a mini-network who urged the producers to "do something outrageous," whereupon they created a sitcom in which President Lincoln makes suggestively homosexual overtures to a black aide, and Mrs. Lincoln, complaining of their unsatisfactory love life, makes heterosexual advances to the same aide. Yet (according to still another poll not reported in the *Times*), only a minority of parents have the will or desire to curb their children's viewing; over three-quarters permit their children to watch as much as they like.[26]*

As people get desensitized to repeated and aggravated forms of vulgarity, violence, and promiscuity, their capacity for outrage gets dulled. Yet there are suggestions of the beginnings of a reaction. That the *Times,* the archetype of the liberal media, should be reporting on television as it has been is itself symptomatic of a growing sense of dismay. Universities too, that other stronghold of the dominant culture, are exhibiting signs of restiveness, on the part of students at least. Professors complain of a growing lack of interest in such politically correct causes as feminism and affirmative action. And students are becoming less permissive in their sexual attitudes. In 1990, 51 percent of col-

---

*This tendency is not confined to television. In March 1999, under the title "The Mainstream Flirts With Pornography Chic," the *Times* reported on the latest developments in art, fashion photography, and A-list movies. A week later, reviewing a film festival at the Museum of Modern Art, the headline read: "Yesterday's Erotica, Today's Quaint."[27]

lege freshmen approved of casual sex; in 1998, 40 percent did. In 1990, 62 percent thought that abortion should be legal; in 1998 (perhaps as a result of the controversy over partial-birth abortions), 50 percent did.[28] Students are also becoming more religious. The *Chronicle of Higher Education* reports upon a surge of religious activities on college campuses, a good deal of it New Age spirituality but some of it traditional religion.[29]

These trends are not limited to college students. 94 percent of teenagers say they believe in God, and half attend church more or less regularly, an increasing number doing so of their own accord rather than because of pressure from their parents.[30] Young people are also becoming somewhat disenchanted with their sexual liberation. More than half of girls (though fewer than half of boys) say sex before marriage is wrong, and more than four-fifths of inner-city high school juniors and seniors, asked about the ideal age to begin having sex, gave an age older than when they themselves had begun.[31]

Their elders are also reconsidering the permissiveness of their own youth. More than half of those who now believe that premarital sex is always wrong have themselves had sex before marriage; and a quarter of those who say that sex for a young teenager is always wrong have had sex at that young age.[32] Twenty-five years ago, only one-seventh of those in their twenties said that premarital sex was always wrong; today one-fourth of that generation (now in their forties) share that view. At that time one-third of the twenty-somethings thought divorce should be more difficult to obtain; today almost half of those in their forties do (and almost two-thirds of the population at large, this compared with only half as recently as 1996).[33]

The dominant ethos, then, is still, for the most part, dominant. But a reaction against it is growing—among young people who will shape the culture of the future, and among their elders who have personally experienced the effects of a revolution that promised liberation and brought, all too often, grief.

. . .

The reaction expresses itself in different ways, in the religious revival most conspicuously, but also in more modest forms that feed into the dissident culture. Those who encourage tolerance for "alternative lifestyles"—and not only tolerance but full legitimacy and equality—have in mind the lifestyles favored by the counterculture. But there are other alternatives, traditional lifestyles, that are asserting themselves and even beginning to be reflected in public policies.

The welfare reform act, for example, is not merely an alternative way of administering welfare; it is an attempt to promote a new (or the revival of an old) attitude toward chronic dependency. Educational innovations provide other alternatives: charter schools and the voucher system enable poor parents to do what the rich have always done—opt out of the public school system and send their children to the school of their choice. Implicit in these alternatives is the recognition that the dominant culture will not soon be changed. Welfare will continue, on the state and local if not national level; and the public school system is not likely to be significantly changed in the near future. But these alternatives are important, precisely because they have been legitimized by the state.

Other alternatives do not require the intervention of the state. They require only that the state forbear from intervening. Private schools, including religious schools, have long been available but are now far more numerous than ever and being utilized by different people for different reasons—cultural and moral as well as educational and religious. Jewish day schools, for example, are flourishing as never before; the largest number are still Orthodox, but others are being established for the first time by Conservative and Reform denominations. As many as forty new Jewish schools have been established since 1990, and ten Jewish high schools in one month alone in 1997; there are now more than 600 such schools in the country, enrolling about 200,000 students.[34]

At the college level, it is evangelical institutions that have grown most dramatically. From 1990 to 1996, while the undergraduate enrollment in public colleges increased by only 4 percent and that in private colleges by 5 percent, the student body of evangelical colleges surged by 24 percent. These schools are distinguished as much by their moral and cultural character as by their religious studies. Some, like Indiana Wesleyan (which doubled in size during this period), hold their students to a rigid code that prohibits not only premarital sex and homosexuality but also alcohol, drugs, tobacco, and social dancing. The most highly regarded of these colleges, Calvin College in Michigan, is far more permissive, allowing alcohol (although not on campus), smoking (although not in buildings), and dancing; gay students are admitted and support services provided for them. In many cases, the academic quality of these institutions, which is generally lower than secular ones, is also improving; Calvin College now has half of its students receiving merit scholarships.[35]

A more radical educational alternative is home schooling. In the past decade alone, the number of children taught at home has more than doubled and is growing by about 15 percent a year; that number is now between one and two million. Moreover, home schooling is no longer confined, as it once was, to religious fundamentalists. Dissatisfaction with the public schools, rather than religion, is the main reason now given by parents undertaking that arduous task. (Black professionals constitute one of the fastest-growing groups of home-schoolers.) Home school organizations provide parents with curricula and advice, and a Home School Legal Defense Association serves as a lobbying group and legal defense organization. It was once thought that home-schoolers would lack the credentials for higher education, but they now surpass students in both private and public schools in standardized tests and are being admitted to some of the most prestigious colleges. (A new two-year college is being planned for those who do not want to enter the mainstream colleges.)[36]

Analogous to home schooling is the "TV-free" home. At a time when television is becoming increasingly intrusive and aggressive, many parents are making the deliberate decision not to have television in their homes. Two million households, most of them with children, now practice this form of "cultural abstinence."[37] Another kind of abstinence is sexual abstinence for teenagers, a principle being promoted by secular as well as faith-based organizations as an alternative to those sex education programs that are accompanied by the distribution of condoms. Still another is alcohol abstinence; as more college students are drinking more heavily, so a rival temperance movement has developed on many campuses. (Between 1993 and 1997, the number of nondrinkers rose from 15.6 percent to 19 percent, while the number of heavy drinkers rose from almost 23 percent to almost 28 percent.)[38] Yet another alternative is the home-based business that permits parents (mothers more often than fathers) to work at home, either full-time or part-time. After only two years in existence, the non-profit Home Business Institute has more than 50,000 members.[39]

Even the universities provide alternatives, places of refuge for dissidents. Like the media, the academic vanguard is constantly "pushing the envelope." The subhead of an article in the *New York Times Magazine* reads: "Porn theory and queer scholarship were last year's college news. The latest academic trend: whiteness studies."[40] Before whiteness studies (which celebrate "white trash" and expose the inherent racism in being white), before porn studies (which are now taught at major universities, accompanied by performances by porn stars), before queer studies (which go beyond gay and lesbian studies to include bisexuality, transvestitism, and other sexual "orientations"), before cultural studies (which analyze comic books and sitcoms with all the solemnity once devoted to Shakespeare and Milton), there were all the other brave new heresies that are now well-established academic orthodoxies. Yet here too, in the midst of the pursuit of the novel and the trivial, there are oases of traditional study where professors and students understand knowledge to be something other than a "social construct" or struggle for "hegemony," and where they do not feel bound by the constraints of the race/class/gender trinity.

The dissident culture is obviously not a cure for the diseases incident to a democratic society. But it is a way of containing and mitigating those diseases. Moreover, it does so in an eminently democratic fashion. Consisting of people of different and overlapping interests and ideas, its only common denominator is the desire to protect and promote values that have been subverted by the dominant culture. Nor is there anything coercive about its composition or recruitment. It is entirely voluntary, its members being free to move in or out at will. Indeed, many have dual citizenship, as it were, belonging to both cultures at different times or straddling both, depending upon the issue and the occasion.

If the dissident culture is self-selecting and self-sustaining, it is not self-sufficient. It is not immune from the diseases afflicting society; the dominant culture is too pervasive and powerful. Nor would it want to immunize itself entirely, even if that were possible. There is too much of value in the dominant culture to warrant the kind of segregation or quarantine that that would require. Those who partially opt out of the culture by one alternative or another are fully aware of the drawbacks of this strategy. Home schooling, school vouchers, even private schools are defensive measures, a last resort against a flawed public school system that was once the pride of our democracy. And the parents of TV-deprived children have good reason to worry about the "forbidden fruit" syndrome.

TV "abstainers" have been called "a band of internal

exiles,"[41] recalling the "inner emigration" of dissidents in Nazi Germany who managed to retreat to some private haven where they were only minimally complicitous with the regime. But the image is deceptive, as is the implication that they are fleeing from a totalitarian regime. So far from being relegated to some segregated enclave in society, those who choose to bypass or abstain from one or another aspect of the dominant culture remain active members of society and the polity—perhaps more active, precisely because they find themselves in a position of dissent. A Department of Education survey finds that the families whose children attend private or parochial schools or are educated at home are more, not less, involved in civic affairs (voting, doing volunteer work, participating in communal activities) than are families in the public school system.[42]

When Paul Weyrich, disappointed by the outcome of the impeachment trial of President Clinton, evoked the idea of political exile, it was promptly repudiated by other leaders of the religious right. Having given the title "Moral Majority" to Jerry Falwell's organization two decades ago, Weyrich decided that since, in his view, a moral majority no longer existed, the time had come to "separate ourselves from this hostile culture" and create "some sort of quarantine" (he gave the example of home schooling) to ensure that "we and our children are not infected." He prefaced his remarks by saying that he was not proposing that "we all become Amish or move to Idaho"; and in a clarifying statement the following day he insisted that he was "not surrendering," only "opening up a different front," a non-political front.[43] But these assurances did not satisfy most of his colleagues, who rejected any suggestion that they withdraw from society or abandon the political struggle.

In fact, religious conservatives have always prided themselves on their devotion to "God and country"—to country as much as God. Those identified with the religious right have been found to be "among the most unwavering in their commitment to the American political system": 85 percent "support our system of government," compared with 65 percent of the public at large; 71 percent take pride in living "under our political system," compared with 61 percent of the whole; 68 percent feel strongly that "our system of government is the best possible system," compared with 53 percent of the whole. Even on the subject of "respect for the political institutions in America," where one might expect most disaffection, they outrank the public by 48 percent to 33 percent.[44] Many are distressed, to be sure, by the present condition of the political culture and exercise their right to dissent from it. But they are loyal to America as a country, a nation, and a polity.

The two cultures, then, are not utterly separate and disparate, but neither are they entirely conformable and reconcilable. Society is polarized in significant ways, and those who deny or minimize this polarization are obscuring the reality—a reality that emerges in one poll after another about one important issue after another. This denial has been made most provocatively by Alan Wolfe in *One Nation, After All*, a title somewhat belied by the subtitle, "What Middle-Class Americans Really Think About . . ." (and which might have been further qualified to read "200 suburban middle class Americans," for that is the scope of this "one nation").[45] Even in his own sparse sample, Wolfe registers some strong differences of opinion on important subjects. Thus 100 of his respondents agree that "America has become far too atheistic and needs a return to strong religious belief," while 79 disagree with that proposition; or 73 believe that same-sex marriage should be legal, while 98 think it should not.[46] What most impresses Wolfe, and what he takes to be the dominant trait of middle-class Americans, is their "nonjudgmentalism," which they (and he) equate with "tolerance."

Wolfe makes it clear, however, that he himself, like most of his respondents by his account, is not tolerant of "absolutist" or "extremist" moral and religious beliefs. He is pleased to find that his middle-class Americans rarely use the kinds of terms he associates with "conservative Christians"—"sin," "moral rot," "decay," "Satan," "infidel."[47]* And he is candid about his own fear that such Christians are a threat to others. "I could not help but feel that this country remains sufficiently religious—and sufficiently Christian—that one needs to worry about the rights of nonbelievers." This may be all the more worrisome because believers can seem plausible and reasonable. "They have arguments on their side, and, even more important, those arguments are lodged not in blind acceptance, but in a liberal language of inclusion and accommodation."[49]

Wolfe's uneasiness with "conservative Christians" did not grow out of the empirical study of *One Nation*. In his earlier book *Whose Keeper?*, he was no less distrustful of them and even more dismissive of religion in general. "Religion," he then announced, "is no longer the source of moral authority it once was." For "rules of moral obligation," he advised, we should look neither to religion nor to philosophy but to "social scientists." Moreover, the "moral vision" of religious conservatives is dangerous as well as obsolete, for it is "so confining in its calls for blind obedience to a handed-down moral code that it would negate all the gains of freedom that modern people have acquired."[50] In an interview after the publication of *One Nation*, Wolfe equated a religious-based morality with the censorious Puritans in *The Scarlet Letter* and the murderous zealots in Bosnia and Northern Ireland.[51]

It is a beguiling picture of suburban middle-class America

---

*It is odd that Wolfe did not hear the word "decay" more often. In a larger survey conducted by the Gallup Institute about the same time, three-quarters of those polled who were *not* of the religious right said that the main cause of America's problems was "moral decay."[48] It is even odder that Wolfe should have found "most striking" the absence of the term "infidel," a word not in the common discourse of Americans.

that we get in this "one nation" scenario—an America of "quiet faith" and near-absolute tolerance.* In this America, we are told, the "culture war" is fought "primarily by intellectuals, not by most Americans themselves."[53] This is not, however, the America, even the middle-class suburban America, that emerges from other polls or even from Wolfe's own data, where not only intellectuals but the people are shown to have serious differences of opinion about basic moral values, differences that cannot be papered over by invoking the words "nonjudgmental" or "tolerance." Nor can they be reconciled by The Eleventh Commandment proposed by one of Wolfe's respondents, "Thou shalt not judge," nor by interpreting the Ten Commandments as "Ten Suggestions," which Wolfe takes to be "the tone in which most middle-class Americans believe we ought to establish moral rules."[54] If this were true, it would itself be evidence of a profound "ethics gap" between those Americans (and not only religious conservatives) who still regard the Ten Commandments as an abiding moral code and those who would demote it to the status of "Ten Suggestions."

A very different view of America emerges from the work of James Davison Hunter, the coauthor of *The State of Disunion,* which documents the cultural and moral divisions in American society.[55] In an earlier book, *Culture Wars,* Hunter analyzed the "competing moral visions" and "cultural systems" reflected in the culture wars and manifested in both the public and private spheres.[56] In a more recent essay, Hunter distinguishes the different levels at which these opposing visions and systems express

---

*Only near-absolute tolerance, for his respondents were not only intolerant of "extremist" religious and moral views; they were not altogether tolerant, Wolfe regretfully reported, of homosexuality. Although a majority "tolerated" it, in a passive sense, nearly three times as many "condemned" it as "positively" accepted it.[52]

themselves: the battles over particular policies, such as abortion, multiculturalism, gay rights, school vouchers, and the like; the "competing moral ideals of how citizens ought to order and maintain public life" which underlie these policy battles; and, more fundamental still, the different metaphysical principles implicit in those ideals—on the one hand, objective standards about what is good and true, "how we should live, and who we are," and on the other, conditional or relative standards derived from personal experience, autonomy, and choice. While many Americans, Hunter concludes, occupy a "middle ground" on policy issues, the basic moral and philosophical disagreements persist, and it is these that are at the root of the culture wars.[57]

Like Hunter, the Catholic philosopher and social critic George Weigel does not hesitate to describe the present situation as a "culture war"—a culture war, but not, as the commentator Patrick Buchanan would have it, a "religious war." The two ideas, Weigel says, are very different. "A culture war can be adjudicated, and a reasonable accommodation reached, through the processes (including electoral and juridical processes) of democratic persuasion; a 'religious war' cannot." The pluralism inherent in E pluribus unum depends upon two circumstances: the understanding that persuasion is preferable to violence; and a "democratic etiquette" that does not dilute or blunt differences of belief but does express them civilly—a "civility," Weigel reminds us, that is not the same as "docility." This democratic etiquette also presupposes a "grammatical ecumenicity," requiring religious thinkers to translate their religiously grounded moral claims into a language and imagery of universal truths based on natural law rather than on divine revelation or ecclesiastical dogma.[58]

From another "grammatical" perspective, the sociologist Peter Berger translates the culture war into a "societywide normative conflict" that pervades the most private and the most public concerns.

This does not mean, of course, that everyone in the country is manning the opposing barricades; this is not the case at all (and is one of the grounds for optimism as to the final outcome). But the battle lines are clearly drawn. Both the democratic political process and the courts are favored battlefields, as each side tries to enlist the vast powers of the state on its behalf. There is a good deal of irony in this development—a relatively recent one, being only some three decades old. America long prided itself as the shining exemplar of successful pluralism. . . . This very pluralism has now generated a deeply divisive conflict of beliefs and values.[59]

If there is something ironic about a culture war in a pluralistic country like America, the war itself, Berger points out, is not unique to America. "The American case," he says, is "paradigmatic," containing the essential elements of all normative conflicts reflected in personal morality, public policies, religions, institutions, and interests. In one form or another, that war is being waged in Western and Eastern Europe, in the Middle East and Far East, in Africa and Latin America. In each country, the conflict is over the nature of the national community and identity, "over just what 'we' are." In this international perspective, the American "case" emerges clearly, not as an unprecedented anomaly, but as an all-too-common phenomenon. And here, as elsewhere, the culture war confronts us with the problem of determining (as the title of Berger's book has it) "the limits of social cohesion" and the means of "conflict and mediation."[60]

In these works, as in those of many other commentators, the culture war is placed in a context that allows for rational and civil discourse without minimizing the gravity of the issues at stake or the depth of the disagreements about them. If there are, as Berger suggests, "limits of social cohesion," there also are means of resolving and mediating conflicts—notably, tolerance and compromise. Tolerance itself, as Michael Walzer has shown, encompasses a range of attitudes, from a resigned acceptance of differences, to a benign indifference to differences, to a stoical accommodation to differences, to a positive curiosity about differences, to an enthusiastic endorsement of differences.[61] In some of these modes, it comes close to what is properly called "nonjudgmentalism"—the familiar "Who is to say what is right and wrong." In others, however, it retains a strong sense of judgment, of firm moral principles and practices, accompanied by the recognition that society requires, as a matter of prudence and civility, a toleration of other principles and practices.* On a few issues—abortion, most notably—the tolerance of both sides is sorely tried, religious conservatives being intolerant of infanticide, as they see it, and liberals (like Walzer himself) being no less intolerant of any infringement of "female autonomy and gender equality."[63] But most issues do not elicit this degree of passion or conviction and are amenable to tolerance and compromise.

The cause of tolerance, however, is not well served by those who pride themselves on their tolerance while identifying religious conservatives with a zeal for persecution reminiscent of the Puritans of old or the fanatics in Bosnia and Northern Ireland. Nor is the cause of compromise furthered by replacing the "Ten Commandments" with "Ten Suggestions," which is not,

---

*The confusion in the meaning of "tolerance" (or perhaps the ambivalence of many people) is reflected in two polls taken little more than a week apart by the same pollsters. In the first, 70 percent said that "we should be more tolerant of people who choose to live according to their own moral standards even if we think they are wrong." In the second, 66 percent said they would be worried if the country becomes "too tolerant of behaviors that are bad for society."[62] (This confusion also obscures the distinction between "tolerance," connoting an attitude, and "toleration," a practice or institutional arrangement. By now the two terms have become interchangeable.)

in fact, a compromise but a capitulation to an all too familiar relativism.*

It is common these days to deplore the expression "culture war," as if the very term is uncivil and inflammatory, a slander upon a good, decent, pacific people. It should hardly need saying that the "culture war" is a "war" only metaphorically, just as the "cultural revolution" is a "revolution" only metaphorically. And metaphors, while not to be taken literally, do serve a serious purpose. There is an important sense—a metaphorical sense, to be sure—in which Americans have lived through such a revolution and are experiencing such a war. To deny either is to belie or trivialize much of the history of the past three decades. It is not surprising that the impeachment trial of President Clinton elicited, from commentator after commentator, references to the culture war, or that, in the midst of this controversy, two-thirds of the public found that "Americans are greatly divided when it comes to the most important values."[64]

Americans can justly pride themselves on surviving both the cultural revolution and the culture war without paroxysms of persecution or bloodshed, without, indeed, serious social strife. For all their differences, the "two cultures" remain firmly fixed within "one nation."

---

*Shortly after Wolfe's book appeared, another made its way onto the best-seller list and remained there for many months: Laura Schlessinger's *The Ten Commandments*. It would appear that a considerable number of Americans (and of literate, book-buying Americans) are still partial to that old concept.

EPILOGUE:
SOME MODEST PREDICTIONS

Historians have not been notably successful in predicting the future. They are not even, a wit has said, very good at predicting the past. Some observers of the religious revival predicted its demise in the late 1980s following the sexual scandals involving two prominent evangelical preachers and the disbandment by Jerry Falwell of the Moral Majority. The radical historian Sean Wilentz gleefully pronounced: "Rarely in modern times has a movement of such reputed magnitude and political potential self-destructed so suddenly. Free thinkers may want to reconsider their skepticism about divine intervention."[1] The political analyst Kevin Phillips was similarly confident that Falwell's farewell was simply a "ratification of a political tide that's come and gone."[2] They were woefully wrong. The Moral Majority had no sooner dissolved than the Christian Coalition appeared on the scene, and with it a host of new organizations and personalities. As the history of American revivalism has shown, such movements do not depend upon a single group or leader. Revivalism, like evangelicalism, is notably populist and fissiparous.[3]

Other historians have predicted that the current revival, the Fourth Great Awakening, will transform the ethos, culture, and even polity of the United States as did the Great Awakenings of the eighteenth and nineteenth centuries.⁴ I have far more modest expectations. I think the revival will continue to invigorate and expand the dissident culture, and influence the dominant culture in myriad ways, without succeeding in converting the country as a whole. If there will be no mass conversion, however, there will be individual conversions. And if not on all the issues that separate the cultures, then at least on some important ones.

I also predict that the religious-*cum*-moral revival will become increasingly moral rather than religious. This is what happened in the past, in each of the Great Awakenings in the United States and, more conspicuously, in the Methodist and Evangelical movements in England in the nineteenth century. As religious groups begin to feel more self-confident and less beleaguered, they tend to shed some of their sectarianism and intransigence. This is already taking place. Witness the shift in tactics among many religious conservatives from advocacy of a constitutional amendment reversing *Roe v. Wade* to a policy designed to chip away at abortion incrementally (by abolishing partial-birth abortions, requiring parental notification, or mandating consultation). A more ecumenical spirit is also evident in the alliances among traditionalists of all faiths on matters of common concern—and not only across faiths but beyond them, to individuals and groups of a purely secular disposition. This was anticipated decades ago when the new religious right made common cause with the old secular "New Right." Inaugurating what was optimistically called the Moral Majority, Jerry Falwell appealed to "fundamentalists, Protestants, Roman Catholics, Jews, Mormons, and persons of no particular religious convictions at all who believe in the moral principles we espouse."⁵

This is still the aim of most dissidents: to bring together people of all religious creeds—and of none—to arrest the moral decline that they (and, indeed, most Americans) see in the culture. This is not an easy task. Counterrevolutions are more difficult to start and sustain than revolutions. Moreover, they never entirely succeed in reversing revolutions. Nor should they; there are always aspects of the revolution that are deemed worthy of preservation. And cultural revolutions are least susceptible to reversal. Victorian England was a rare case of such a reversal, under conditions very different from those present today. The religious revival was then far more extensive in scope, and the moral revival was unhindered by the distractions and enticements of an affluent economy, a mobile society, and a highly individualistic culture.

But if a counterrevolution is unlikely, a more modest reformation is not. There are already signs of this, as more and more people leave the state of denial in which they have so long taken refuge and begin to acknowledge the gravity of the problems confronting us. This is the meaning of the consensus about "moral decline." It is not only conservatives (religious and secular) who now deplore the breakdown of the family; liberals do as well, responding to the irrefutable evidence of the consequences of that breakdown. And no one, liberal or conservative, seriously disputes the prevalence (even glorification) of violence, vulgarity, and promiscuity in videos and rap music, or denies their degrading effects on young people in particular. Nor does anyone now say of television, as was once said of books, that "no one was ever corrupted by it"—a dubious argument even applied to books, still more to television, which is obviously a much more potent source of corruption. Nor does anyone anymore (as did Timothy Leary and other devotees of LSD in the 1960s) celebrate the glories of "mind-expanding drugs." Nor do many people today seriously doubt the inadequacies of education at all levels, or the fragility of communal ties, or the coarsening and debasement of the culture, or the "defining down" of morality, public and private. It is no mean achievement to have reached at least this point of consensus about some of the "diseases incident to democratic society."

There has even been some convergence on the remedies for these diseases. The enthusiasm with which liberals and conservatives, religious and secular people, politicians and academics, have embraced the idea of civil society testifies not only to the widespread recognition of the gravity of the diseases but also to a search for remedies in the mediating institutions of communities, churches, and voluntary groups. And just as the study of civil society has become a growth industry in the past few years, so has the study of the family, both subjects now being exposed to more rigorous, hard-headed analysis than was evident in the first wave of enthusiasm and euphoria. We have also witnessed a good deal of bold rethinking about crime, welfare, education, the role of private associations, and the relation of church and state, resulting in significant changes of values and attitudes as well as new programs and policies. Proposals that would once have been dismissed as politically suicidal, the famous "third rails" of American politics (the reform of social security, for example), have turned out to be not nearly so lethal as had been thought, encouraging us to explore still other venturous measures to cope with the disorders of society.

In addressing, seriously and imaginatively, the moral and cultural condition of society, we have also learned (or some of us have) to temper our rhetoric. The "hell in a handbasket" epithet hardly describes those who recognize that much has been accomplished and much remains to be done. Nor do the old labels, pessimist and optimist, apply to those who are neither apocalyptic nor utopian, who do not think of themselves as either at the nadir of Western civilization or at the zenith of a brave new world, and who do not aspire to solve all problems but only to mitigate some of them.

One final prediction: If the religious-*cum*-moral revival does become attenuated in its religiosity, and if the dissident culture comes to be more and more defined by its moral rather than religious character, there may come a time when historians will have to remind their contemporaries (as we have been reminded in our own time) that they are living off the religious capital of a previous generation and that that capital is being perilously depleted. The dynamics of the situation—the gradual secularization and liberalization of the dissident culture itself—may even result in a relaxation of its moral as well as religious temper, so that it eventually loses its distinctive quality and purpose. We may then find ourselves caught up in yet another cycle of de-moralization and re-moralization, including, perhaps, another Great Awakening.

But such prophecies take us far into the future. For the moment, let us be content with the knowledge that the two cultures are living together with some degree of tension and dissension but without civil strife or anarchy. America has a long tradition of tolerance which has seen it through far more divisive periods than the present, a tolerance that does not require, as is sometimes supposed, a diminution of conviction but that is entirely consistent with the strongest convictions. It is this kind of tolerance that serves as a mediating force between the two cultures, assuaging tempers and subduing passions, while respecting the very real, very important differences between them. If we cannot foresee, in the near future, a dramatic reunion of the two cultures or a total reformation of society, we may look forward to more modest achievements—at the very least to an abatement of the diseases incident to democratic society.

NOTES

PREFACE

1. Fernand Braudel, "Personal Testimony," *Journal of Modern History*, Dec. 1972, p. 454.

CHAPTER I
A HISTORICAL PROLOGUE: THE "VICES OF LEVITY"
AND THE "DISEASES OF DEMOCRACY"

1. Adam Smith, *An Inquiry into the Nature and Causes of the Wealth of Nations*, ed. Edwin Cannan (New York [Modern Library ed.], 1937), pp. 746–7.
2. Ibid., p. 748.
3. Hippolyte Taine, *Notes on England*, trans. and ed. Edward Hyams (London, 1957 [orig. Fr. ed., 1860–70]), p. 12. (The proclamation was cited by Taine in his notes written during his visit to London in 1862. The quotation given here is Hyams's retranslation from Taine's French.)
4. For a discussion of Victorian virtues and vices, see Gertrude Himmelfarb, *The De-Moralization of Society: From Victorian Virtues to Modern Values* (New York, 1995).
5. John Maynard Keynes, *Two Memoirs* (New York, 1949), p. 97.

6. *The Letters of Virginia Woolf,* vol. II (1912–22), ed. Nigel Nicolson and Joanne Trautmann (New York, 1976), p. 293.

7. Virginia Woolf, *A Writer's Diary: Being Extracts from the Diary of Virginia Woolf,* ed. Leonard Woolf (London, 1953), p. 47 (Aug. 16, 1922).

8. *Federalist Papers,* 55.

9. Matthew Arnold, "Civilisation in the United States" (1888), in *Five Uncollected Essays,* ed. Kenneth Allott (Liverpool, 1953), p. 46. (This is not a direct quotation from the traveler, Sir Lepel Griffin, but Arnold's paraphrase of it.)

10. Lionel Trilling, *Matthew Arnold* (New York, 1949), p. 398. (This is Trilling's paraphrase of Whitman.)

11. David Hall, "The Victorian Connection," in *Victorian America,* ed. Daniel Walker Howe (Philadelphia, 1976), pp. 81–2.

12. Daniel Walker Howe, "Victorian Culture in America," in ibid., p. 4.

13. William J. Novak, *The People's Welfare: Law and Regulation in Nineteenth-Century America* (Chapel Hill, N. C., 1996), p. 1.

14. Henry F. May, *The End of American Innocence: A Study of the First Years of Our Own Time 1912–1917* (Oxford, Eng., 1979 [1st ed., 1959]), p. ix. About the same time, William E. Leuchtenburg spoke of the 1920s as "the revolution in morals." (*The Perils of Prosperity,* 1914–32 [Chicago, 1958], p. 158.

15. Virginia Woolf, *Moments of Being: Unpublished Autobiographical Writings,* ed. Jeanne Schulkind (New York, 1976), p. 163.

16. May, p. x.

17. "A Freeze-Out" (1931), in *The Short Stories of F. Scott Fitzgerald,* ed. Matthew J. Bruccoli (New York, 1989), p. 649.

18. F. Scott Fitzgerald, *This Side of Paradise* (New York, 1948 [1st ed., 1920]), p. 60.

19. Kevin White, *The First Sexual Revolution: The Emergence of Male Heterosexuality in Modern America* (New York, 1993). See also James R. McGovern, "The American Woman's Pre-World War I Freedom in Manners and Morals," *Journal of American History,* 1968, pp. 315–33; John C. Burnham, "The Progressive Era Revolution in American Attitudes toward Sex," ibid., 1973, pp. 885–908.

20. Robert S. Lynd and Helen Merrell Lynd, *Middletown: A Study in American Culture* (New York, 1956 [1st ed., 1928]), p. 112. Kevin White cites statistics suggesting a far more radical change in sexual mores. "Women born after 1900 were two and a half times more

likely to have had sex before marriage than those born before."
(White, p. 15) But the source for that figure, as for most of the
others cited by White, is Alfred Kinsey's *Sexual Behavior in the
Human Female*, a dubious authority.

21. Joseph A. Schumpeter, *Capitalism, Socialism and Democracy* (3d ed.,
New York, 1950), p. 143

22. John Stuart Mill, *Principles of Political Economy* (Toronto, 1965 [1st
ed., 1848]), II, 752 ff.

23. Pitirim A. Sorokin, *The American Sex Revolution* (Boston, 1956),
pp. 23, 45.

24. Daniel Bell, *The Cultural Contradictions of Capitalism* (New York,
1976).

25. Lionel Trilling, *Beyond Culture: Essays on Literature and Learning*
(New York, 1965), pp. xii–xv.

26. Theodore Roszak, "Youth and the Great Refusal," *The Nation*,
March 25, 1968, p. 406.

27. Roszak, *The Making of a Counter Culture: Reflections on the Techno-
cratic Society and Its Youthful Opposition* (Berkeley, 1995 [1st ed.,
1970]), pp. xl–xli.

28. Christopher Lasch, *The Culture of Narcissism: American Life in an
Age of Diminishing Expectations* (New York, 1979).

29. Glenn C. Loury, "The Moral Quandary of the Black Community," *Public Interest*, Spring 1985.

30. See Arthur Marwick, *The Sixties: Cultural Revolution in Britain,
France, Italy, and the United States, c.1958–c.1974* (Oxford, Eng.,
1998).

31. *State of the Union: America in the 1990s*, ed. Reynolds Farley (New
York, Russell Sage Foundation, 1995), II, 15 (citing U.S. Bureau of
the Census, Statistical Abstract of the United States, 1993); Con-
stance Sorrentino, "The Changing Family in International Perspective," *Monthly Labor Review*, March 1990. For more recent
figures, see the *Economist*, Sept. 26, 1998 (citing Eurostat and the
U.S. Department of Commerce).

32. *Federalist Papers* 10.

33. In one survey, 76 percent of "other Americans" (i.e., not of the
"religious right") said that the main cause of America's problems
is "moral decay"; 88 percent of the religious right gave that
answer. (American Jewish Committee, "A Survey of the Religious Right," p. 8 [conducted by the Gallup International Institute, May 10–June 3, 1996].) Another poll the same year by Daniel

Yankelovich had as many as 87 percent of the public distressed by the moral condition of the country (cited in the Institute for American Values, "A Call to Civil Society" [New York, 1998], p. 4). In 1998, with the economy in a state of near-euphoria, 60 to 75 percent said that the country has declined in "moral and ethical standards," that they were troubled by this "moral decline," and that the country was "going on the wrong track" in terms of values. (*Public Perspective*, Roper Center, Feb./Mar. 1998, p. 12. See also *Washington Post*, July 14, 1998, p. A8 [citing *Washington Post*/ABC poll]; *Washington Post*, Sept. 11, 1998, p. A40 [citing *Washington Post*/Kaiser Family Foundation/Harvard University poll]); CNN/Gallup, Feb. 4–8, 1999.)

34. Everett Carll Ladd and Karlyn H. Bowman, *What's Wrong: A Survey of American Satisfaction and Complaint* (AEI Press, Washington, D.C., 1998), p. 40. See also David Whitman, *The Optimism Gap: The I'm OK–They're Not Syndrome and the Myth of American Decline* (New York, 1998).

35. *Crime in the United States 1997*, Uniform Crime Reports, U.S. Department of Justice, F.B.I., p. 66; *Sourcebook of Criminal Justice Statistics 1997*, U.S. Department of Justice, p. 294. See also M. Sickmund, H. Snyder, and E. Poe-Yamagat, *Juvenile Offenders and Victims: 1997 Update on Violence*, Office of Juvenile Justice and Delinquency Prevention, U.S. Department of Justice, 1997. These figures continued to fall in 1998, according to the preliminary Uniform Crime Reports (released May 16, 1999).

36. James Alan Fox and Marianne W. Zawitz, "Homicide Trends in the United States," Bureau of Justice Statistics, FBI, Jan. 1999; FBI Supplementary Homicide Reports, 1976–97; *New York Times*, Dec. 29, 1998, p. A16 (updated by New York Police Department, reported in the *Washington Post*, Jan. 1, 1999, p. A25). Using a different methodology, the preliminary Uniform Crime Reports (released May 16, 1999) has 633 homicides in New York City in 1998.

37. "Aid to Families with Dependent Children and Temporary Assistance," updated Dec. 1998, Administration for Children and Families, U.S. Department of Health and Human Services (released April 1999).

38. Monthly Vital Statistics Report, supplement 1998, National Center for Health Statistics. (For black women the rate fell from 94 to 74.)

39. S. J. Ventura, S. C. Curtin, and T. J. Mathews, "Teenage Births in the United States: National and State Trends, 1990–96," and "Births:

Final Data for 1997," National Center for Health Statistics, 1998 and 1999. For black teenagers the rate fell from 115.5 to 91.7. Teenage pregnancies (as distinct from births) declined from 117.1 per thousand in 1990 to 101.1 in 1995. ("U.S. Teenage Pregnancy Statistics," Alan Guttmacher Institute, 1998.)

40. "1995 National Survey of Family Growth," National Center for Health Statistics, 1997; J. C. Abma, A. Chandra, W. D. Mosher, L. Peterson, and L. Piccino, "Fertility, Family Planning, and Women's Health: New Data from the 1995 National Survey of Family Growth," National Center for Health Statistics, 1997.

41. Advance Report of Final Divorce Statistics, 1989–90, National Center for Health Statistics; National Vital Statistics Reports, Nov. 4, 1998, National Center for Health Statistics.

42. Stanley K. Henshaw, "Abortion Incidence and Services in the United States, 1995–1996," *Family Planning Perspectives* (Alan Guttmacher Institute, 1998), p. 264.

43. Burt Solomon, "Teens and Sex," *National Journal*, July 4, 1998, p. 1566.

44. M. D. Resnick, P. S. Bearman, R. W. Blum, et al., "Protecting Adolescents From Harm: Findings from the National Longitudinal Study on Adolescent Health," *Journal of the American Medical Association*, Sept. 1997.

45. Patricia Donovan, "Falling Teen Pregnancy Birthrates: What's Behind the Decline?" *The Guttmacher Report on Public Policy*, Oct. 1998, p. 4.

46. National Center for Health Statistics, 1998 and 1999. Teenage births had been far more numerous in the 1950s, but the vast majority were to married women, reflecting the fact that many more women then got married in their late teens.

47. Michael Lind, *Up From Conservatism: Why the Right Is Wrong for America* (New York, 1996), p. 169; Christopher Jencks, "Is the American Underclass Growing?" in *The Urban Underclass*, ed. Jencks and Paul E. Peterson (Brookings Institution Press, Washington, D.C., 1991), p. 87.

48. U.S. Census Bureau report, Dec. 1998.

48. Henshaw, "Abortion Incidence," p. 13.

50. Report by Joyce Abma (of the National Center for Health Statistics) and Freya L. Sonenstein (of the Urban Institute), "Teenage Sexual Behavior and Contraceptive Use: An Update," chart 3 (April 28, 1998); "Teen Sex and Pregnancy," items 12–17, Alan

Guttmacher Institute; Douglas J. Besharov and Karen N. Gardiner, "Trends in Teen Sexual Behavior," *Children and Youth Services Review*, 1997, pp. 343–7; Patricia Donovan, "Falling Teen Pregnancy, Birthrates: What's Behind the Decline?," Alan Guttmacher Institute report, Oct. 1998.

51. Kay S. Hymowitz, "Tweens: Ten Going on Sixteen," *City Journal*, Autumn 1998, pp. 26–39.

52. U.S. Census Bureau report, July 1998; Larry L. Bumpass and Hsin-Hen, "Trends in Cohabitation and Implications for Children's Family Contexts," unpublished manuscript, Center for Demography, University of Michigan, 1998; Larry L. Bumpass and James A. Sweet, "Cohabitation, Marriage and Union Stability: Preliminary Findings from NSFH2" (National Survey of Families and Households, 2d wave, May 1995), p. 7. See also Bumpass and Sweet, "The Role of Cohabitation in Declining Rates of Marriage," *Journal of Marriage and the Family*, Nov. 1991, p. 921; Alfred DeMaris and K. Vaninadha Rao, "Premarital Cohabitation and Subsequent Marital Stability in the United States: A Reassessment," in ibid., Feb. 1992, p. 178; Alfred DeMaris and William MacDonald, "Premarital Cohabitation and Marital Instability: A Test of the Unconventionality Hypothesis," in ibid., May 1993; Steven L. Nock, "A Comparison of Marriages and Cohabiting Relationships," *Journal of Family Issues*, Jan. 1995; Zheng Wu, "Premarital Cohabitation and Postmarital Cohabiting Union Formation," in ibid., March 1995.

53. L. D. Johnston, P. M. O'Malley, and J. G. Bachman, "National Survey Results on Drug Use from the Monitoring the Future Study, 1975–1997," National Institute on Drug Abuse, U.S. Department of Health and Human Services. The use of heroin by teenagers has doubled between 1990 and 1996; while the number is still relatively small (1.8 percent), it is troubling because of the addictive nature and consequences of that drug. (*New York Times*, Dec. 8, 1998, p. A20, citing the Dec. 1998 issue of the journal *Pediatrics*.)

54. *Health, United States, 1998*, Vital Statistics of the United States (National Center for Health Statistics), vol. II, part A, pp. 243–4.

55. Fox and Zawitz, "Homicide Trends." (See note 36 above.)

56. James Alan Fox, "Trends in Juvenile Violence: 1997 Update," Office of Justice Programs, U.S. Department of Justice, 1998. The violent crime rate for juveniles has been consistently higher than that of adults. Between 1990 and 1996, while the crime rate for adults had already started to decline, that of youths aged fifteen to

twenty rose by 5 percent and of those fourteen and under by as much as 15 percent. (I am indebted for these statistics to Patrick A. Langan, Senior Research Analyst of the Bureau of Justice Statistics in the Department of Justice.)

57. Mary Ann Lamanna and Agnes Riedmann, *Marriage and Families: Making Choices in a Diverse Society* (6th ed.; Belmont, Calif., 1997), p. 8; Monthly Vital Statistics Report, supplement 1998, National Center for Health Statistics; *Public Perspective*, Oct./Nov. 1997, p. 9.

58. The black ratio in 1965 was 24.5 percent. Today it is 22 percent for white non-Hispanics, 32.4 percent for the country at large, and 69 percent for blacks. (The black ratio declined slightly from 70 percent in 1994.)

59. National Center for Health Statistics. See also Barbara Dafoe Whitehead, *The Divorce Culture* (New York, 1997); William Galston, "Divorce American Style," *Public Interest*, Summer 1996, p. 14; Robert H. Lauer and Jeanette C. Lauer, *Marriage and Family: Diversity and Strengths* (Mountain View, Calif., 1994).

60. See note 40 above.

61. Fox and Zawitz, "Homicide Trends." (See note 36 above.)

62. Roger Shattuck, "When Evil Is Cool," *Atlantic Monthly*, Jan. 1999, p. 78.

63. Myron Magnet, *The Dream and the Nightmare: The Sixties' Legacy to the Underclass* (New York, 1993).

64. Charles Murray, "The Coming White Underclass," *Wall Street Journal*, Oct. 29, 1993, p. A14.

65. Rochelle Gurstein, *The Repeal of Reticence: A History of America's Cultural and Legal Struggles over Free Speech, Obscenity, Sexual Liberation, and Modern Art* (New York, 1996). See also Wendy Shalit, *A Return to Modesty: Discovering the Lost Virtue* (New York, 1999).

66. John Bayley, *Elegy for Iris* (London, 1998). See Gertrude Himmelfarb, "A Man's Own Household His Enemies," *Commentary*, Jul.–Aug. 1999.

67. Daniel Patrick Moynihan, "Defining Deviancy Down," *American Scholar*, Winter 1993, pp. 17–30.

68. Charles Krauthammer, "Defining Deviancy Up," *New Republic*, Nov. 22, 1993, pp. 20–5.

69. The "new Victorian" or "neo-Victorian" label has been attached to those feminists who favor the prohibition of pornography and the imposition of speech and sexual codes. (See Himmelfarb, *The De-Moralization of Society*, pp. 259–63.) "Neo-puritanism" arose in the course of the debate over the impeachment of

President Clinton. The columnist R. W. Apple, Jr., for example, complained that "the deadly sweep of the scythe of neo-puritanism appears unstoppable." (*New York Times*, Dec. 20, 1998, p. A1.)

70. *Brookings Review,* Spring 1999, p. 15 (citing *Washington Post*/Kaiser Family Foundation/Harvard University poll, 1998).

CHAPTER II

CIVIL SOCIETY: "THE SEEDBEDS OF VIRTUE"

1. In America, the main proponents of this view include John Rawls, Ronald Dworkin, Thomas Nagel, Amy Gutman, Bruce Ackerman, and Stephen Holmes. For a review of this debate, see Gertrude Himmelfarb, "The Unravelled Fabric—And How to Knit It Up," *Times Literary Supplement*, May 17, 1996, pp. 12–13. A recent attempt to mediate between the two positions is Nancy L. Rosenblum's *Membership and Morals: The Personal Uses of Pluralism in America* (Princeton, 1998), which argues for a pluralistic liberalism in which the communities that comprise civil society serve the particular needs and interests of individuals rather than the promotion of civic virtue.

2. See Robert Wuthnow, *Sharing the Journey: Support Groups and America's New Quest for Community* (New York, 1994).

3. *The Basic Works of Aristotle*, ed. Richard McKeon (New York, 1941), p. 1129 (*Politics*, Bk. I, ch. 2).

4. John Locke, *Two Treatises of Government*, ed. Peter Laslett (2d. ed., Cambridge, Eng., 1967), pp. 341, 352. (Second Treatise, pars. 85, 101). (I have modernized the spelling, capitalization, and punctuation.)

5. David Hume, "Of the Origin of Government," in *Political Essays*, ed. Charles W. Hendel (New York, 1953), p. 42.

6. Jean-Jacques Rousseau, *The First and Second Discourses*, ed. Victor Gourevitch (New York, 1986), p. 170.

7. Adam Ferguson, *An Essay on the History of Civil Society*, ed. Duncan Forbes (Edinburgh, 1966), p. 155.

8. Edmund Burke, *Reflections on the Revolution in France* (Dolphin ed., New York, 1961), pp. 48, 72. One can also cite passing references to the term in other classic works of the eighteenth century: Bernard Mandeville, *The Fable of the Bees* (1714) (Penguin ed., London, 1970), p. 95; Adam Smith, *An Inquiry into the Nature and Causes of the Wealth of Nations*, ed. Edwin Cannan (Modern

Library ed., New York, 1937), p. 759; Immanuel Kant, *The Science of Right* (1785), trans. W. Hastie, in *Great Books of the Western World* (Chicago, 1952), XLII, 402.

9. Georg Wilhelm Friedrich Hegel, *Philosophy of Right*, trans. and ed. T. M. Knox (Oxford, Eng., 1952), p. 266 (add. 116 to par. 182); p. 189 (par. 289); p. 267 (add. 116 to par. 182). (These "additions" were culled from Hegel's lecture notes and published in the edition that appeared in 1833, two years after his death.)

10. Alexis de Tocqueville, *De la démocratie en Amérique* (Paris, 1981 [1st ed., 1835]), I, 340; *Democracy in America*, trans. Henry Reeve (London, 1862 [reprint of first ed., 1835]), I, 294.

11. Tocqueville, *Democracy in America*, ed. Phillips Bradley (New York, 1948), I, 251.

12. Tocqueville, *Democracy in America*, ed. J. P. Mayer and Max Lerner, trans. George Lawrence (New York, 1966), p. 225.

13. Hannah Arendt, *The Origins of Totalitarianism* (New York, 1951), pp. 4, 158, 177.

14. Hannah Arendt, *The Human Condition* (Chicago, 1958), pp. 22–78. See also Hanna Fenichel Pitkin, *The Attack of the Blob: Hannah Arendt's Concept of the Social* (Chicago, 1998).

15. It does not appear, for example, in the "Syntopicon" of the *Great Books of the Western World*, ed. Mortimer J. Adler (Chicago, 1975 [lst ed., 1952]); or the *Great Treasury of Western Thought*, ed. Mortimer Adler and Charles Van Doren (New York, 1977); or the *Columbia Encyclopedia* (5th ed., New York, 1993); or the *Encyclopedia of the Social Sciences* (New York, 1937); or the *International Encyclopedia of the Social Sciences* (New York, 1968); or even in the revised edition of the *Oxford English Dictionary* (Oxford, 1989). Nor does it appear in Robert Nisbet's *The Quest for Community* (Oxford, 1953), which is often cited in this literature. (Nisbet is more interested in "community" as a countervailing force to political power than as an instrument of social power.) John Courtney Murray, in *We Hold These Truths: Catholic Reflections on the American Proposition* (New York 1964 [1st ed., 1960], pp. 33–4), uses the term "civil society" in the sense of a "civilized" or "orderly" society, but not to refer to the voluntary associations or mediating institutions of society.

One of the earliest recent attempts to popularize the idea of mediating structures is the 1977 pamphlet by Richard John Neuhaus and Peter L. Berger, *To Empower People,* but even there the term "civil society" does not appear. The book published under that title (AEI Press, Washington, D.C., 1996), which reprints that pamphlet together with essays on the subject, has the subtitle: "From State to Civil Society." The subtitle of the original pamphlet was "The Role of Mediating Structures in Public Policy."

16. Burke, p. 59.

17. Mary Ann Glendon and David Blankenhorn, eds., *Seedbeds of Virtue: Sources of Competence, Character, and Citizenship in American Society* (Lanham, Md., 1995).

18. Michael J. Sandel, *Democracy's Discontent: America in Search of a Public Philosophy* (Cambridge, Mass., 1996), p. 13.

19. Robert Putnam, "Bowling Alone: America's Declining Social Capital," *Journal of Democracy*, January 1995; "The Strange Disappearance of Civic America," *The American Prospect*, Winter 1996; "Tuning In, Tuning Out: The Strange Disappearance of Social Capital in America," *PS: Political Science and Politics*, Dec. 1995; and "Bowling Alone, Revisited," *The Responsive Community*, Spring 1995. Francis Fukuyama has reinterpreted the decline of "social capital" to mean the decline of "social trust." (*Trust: The Social Virtues and the Creation of Prosperity* [New York, 1995].)

20. For the statistical data refuting the Putnam thesis, see *Public Perspective* (Roper Center), June/July 1996; Wuthnow, *Sharing the Journey*. Everett Carll Ladd speaks of the "churning," rather than declining, of civic associations. (*The Ladd Report* [New York, 1999], pp. 4, 25.

21. Alan Wolfe suggests that Americans today are more likely to find civil society not in "neighborhoods, families, and churches," but in "the workplace, in cyberspace, and in [less organized] forms of political participation." ("Is Civil Society Obsolete? Revisiting Predictions of the Decline of Civil Society in *Whose Keeper?*," in *Community Works: The Revival of Civil Society in America*, ed. E. J. Dionne Jr. [Brookings Institution Press, Washington, D.C., 1998], p. 22.)

22. Dan Coats, "Can Congress Revive Civil Society?" *Policy Review*, Jan./Feb. 1996, p. 25.

23. Don Eberly, "Civic Renewal vs. Moral Renewal," *Policy Review*, Sept./Oct. 1998, p. 46. See also Eberly, *America's Promise: Civil Society and the Renewal of American Culture* (Lanham, Md., 1998).

24. Amitai Etzioni, *Sunday Times* (London), Mar. 19, 1995, p. 7. See also Etzioni, *The Spirit of Community: Rights, Responsibilities, and the Communitarian Agenda* (New York, 1993).

25. Alan Ehrenhalt, *The Lost City: Discovering the Forgotten Virtues of Community in the Chicago of the 1950s* (New York, 1995).

26. David Gelernter, *1939: The Lost World of the Fair* (New York, 1995).

27. Ehrenhalt, p. 32.

28. Ibid., p. 270.

29. Ehrenhalt, "Where Have All the Followers Gone?" in *Community Works*, p. 94.

30. Sandel, p. 333. See also Charles Taylor, *Sources of the Self: The Making of the Modern Identity* (Cambridge, Mass., 1989), and William A. Galston, *Liberal Purposes: Goods, Virtues, and Diversity in the Liberal State* (Cambridge, Mass., 1991). Neither in *The Spirit of Community* nor in *The New Golden Rule: Community and Morality in a Democratic Society* (New York, 1996) does Amitai Etzioni confront the subject of the relation of the welfare state to communitarianism.

31. Michael Walzer, *Spheres of Justice: A Defense of Pluralism and Equality* (New York, 1983), p. 36. See also Walzer, "The Communitarian Critique of Liberalism," *Political Theory*, 1990, pp. 15, 20; "Rescuing Civil Society," *Dissent,* Winter 1999.

32. *New York Times*, Jan. 24, 1996, p. A13.

33. John Stuart Mill, *On Liberty* (Everyman ed., London, 1940), p. 72.

34. For example, Charles Murray, *What It Means to Be a Libertarian: A Personal Interpretation* (New York, 1997).

35. Quoted in Andrzej Korbonski, "Civil Society and Democracy in Poland: Problems and Prospects," in *Civil Society, Political Society, Democracy*, ed. Adolf Bibic and Gigi Graziano (Ljubljana, Slovenia, 1994), p. 227.

36. See Krishan Kumar, "Civil Society: An Inquiry into the Usefulness of an Historical Term," *British Journal of Sociology*, Sept. 1993, and the reply and counter-reply to this article in subsequent issues of the journal. See also J. Keane, ed., *Civil Society and the State: New European Perspectives* (London, 1988), especially the article by Z. A. Pelczynski, "Solidarity and 'The Rebirth of Civil Society' in Poland, 1976–81"; Jacques Rupnik, "Dissent in Poland, 1968–78: The End of Revisionism and the Rebirth of Civil Society," in Rudolf Tokes, ed., *Opposition in Eastern Europe* (Baltimore, 1979).

37. Antonio Gramsci, *Prison Notebooks* (New York, 1971 [1st ed., 1947]).

38. See Adam B. Seligman, *The Idea of Civil Society* (New York, 1992), pp. 6 ff.

39. Aleksander Smolar, "From Opposition to Atomization," *Journal of Democracy*, Jan. 1996, pp. 29–30. See also "Rival Visions," excerpts

from the writings and speeches of Václav Havel and Václav Klaus on this subject in the same issue.

40. Václav Havel, "Paradise Lost," *New York Review of Books*, April 9, 1992, p. 6.

CHAPTER III

THE FAMILY: "A MINIATURE SOCIAL SYSTEM"

1. David Popenoe, "The Roots of Declining Social Virtue: Family, Community, and the Need for a 'Natural Communities Policy,'" in *Seedbeds of Virtue: Sources of Competence, Character, and Citizenship in American Society,* ed. Mary Ann Glendon and David Blankenhorn (Lanham, Md., 1995), p. 79.

2. Joseph A. Schumpeter, *Capitalism, Socialism and Democracy* (3d ed., New York, 1950), pp. 156–63.

3. *New York Times*, July 10, 1998, p. A6.

4. Christopher Lasch, *Haven in a Heartless World: The Family Besieged* (New York, 1977), pp. xiv, 8; Richard T. Gill, *Posterity Lost: Progress, Ideology, and the Decline of the American Family* (Lanham, Md., 1997), pp. 22–3, 58–9.

5. J. C. Abma, A. Chandra, W. D. Mosher, L. Peterson, and L. Piccinino, *Fertility, Family Planning, and Women's Health: New Data from the 1995 National Survey of Family Growth*, Vital Health Statistics, National Center for Health Statistics, 1997.

6. L. Lamison-White, *Poverty in the United States: 1996*, Current Population Reports, 1997, U.S. Bureau of Census.

7. *Washington Post*, Aug. 21, 1998, p. A3, and *Wall Street Journal*, Dec. 1, 1998, p. A22 (citing unpublished paper by Cynthia Harper and Sara S. McLanahan presented to American Sociological Association, Aug. 21, 1998). An earlier study came to the same conclusion: "Controlling for family configuration erases the relationship between race and crime and between low income and crime." (Elaine Kamarck and William Galston, *Putting Children First: A Progressive Family Policy for the 1990s* [Progressive Policy Institute, Washington, D.C., 1990], pp. 14–15).

8. Sara McLanahan and Gary Sandefur, *Growing Up with a Single Parent: What Hurts, What Helps* (Cambridge, Mass., 1994), pp. 58–9.

9. *Trends in the Well-Being of America's Children and Youth, 1997*, U.S. Department of Health and Human Services, p. 26. Judith Rich Harris, *The Nurture Assumption: Why Children Turn Out the Way*

They Do (New York, 1998), disputes some of these findings, claiming that it is not the breakup of the family or the fatherless family per se that contributes to these unfortunate effects but other factors, such as poverty, frequency of moving, genetic disposition, or peer pressure. But most of these studies take these factors into account, some of which (poverty or moving) are themselves the consequence of family breakdown. Moreover, family breakdown often occurs in communities where the "peers" are themselves the products of similarly "disintact" families. (For a thoughtful analysis of Harris's book, see Mary Eberstadt, "What Are Parents For?," *Commentary*, Dec. 1998.)

10. David Blankenhorn, *Fatherless America: Confronting Our Most Urgent Social Problem* (New York, 1995), pp. 33, 35, 245 (n.30). See also David Popenoe, *Life Without Father* (New York, 1996), pp. 65–74 and notes pp. 241–3.

11. Ronet Bachman and Linda E. Saltzman, "Violence Against Women: Estimates from the Redesigned Survey," Bureau of Justice Statistics, Aug. 1995, p. 3.

12. *America's Children 1998: Indicators of Children's Well-Being*, Forum on Child and Family Statistics, Centers for Disease Control and Prevention, National Center for Health Statistics.

13. Charles Murray, "The Coming White Underclass," *Wall Street Journal*, Oct. 29, 1993, p. A14; James Q. Wilson, "Bring Back the Orphanage," *Wall Street Journal*, Aug. 22, 1994, p. A10; "The Storm Over Orphanages," *Time*, Dec. 12, 1994, p. 58; Gertrude Himmelfarb, "The Victorians Get a Bad Rap," *New York Times*, Jan. 9, 1995, p. A15.

14. McLanahan and Sandefur, p. 1. See also Don S. Browning, et al., *From Culture Wars to Common Ground: Religion and the American Family Debate* (Louisville, Ky., 1997), pp. 56–8. American sociologists studying longitudinal surveys of British children have found the same psychological disorders associated with the divorce of parents, regardless of income, race, or social status. (Andrew J. Cherlin, P. Lindsay Chase-Lansdale, and Christine McRae, "Effects of Parental Divorce on Mental Health Throughout the Life Course," *American Sociological Review*, April 1998.)

15. Joseph E. Schwartz et al., "Sociodemographic and Psychosocial Factors in Childhood as Predictors of Adult Mortality," *American Journal of Public Health*, Sept. 1995, pp. 1237–42; Howard S. Friedman et al., "Psychosocial and Behavioral Predictors of Longevity," *American Psychologist*, Feb. 1995, pp. 69–78.

16. *Business Week*, March 9, 1998, p. 22 (citing National Center for Health Statistics).
17. "Living Together Fails as Trial Run," *USA Today*, July 13, 1998, p. 13A (citing researchers at Washington State University, University of California at Los Angeles, the University of Denver, and the National Institute of Mental Health).
18. *Lingua Franca*, Oct. 1997, pp. 14–15.
19. Christina Hardyment, "We Are Family," *Prospect*, June 1998, p. 38.
20. Browning, p. 46.
21. Adam Smith, *Lectures on Jurisprudence*, eds. R. L. Meek, D. D. Raphael, and P. G. Stein (Oxford, 1978 [lectures delivered in 1766]), p. 450.
22. Lasch, *Haven in a Heartless World*, p. 14. See also Lasch, *The Culture of Narcissism: American Life in an Age of Diminishing Expectations* (New York, 1979), pp. 154–5.
23. *Los Angeles Times*, Jan. 28, 1998, p. A16 (citing interview on NBC *Today* show).
24. Gill, p. 27.
25. Nicholas Eberstadt, "World Population Implosion?" *Public Interest,* Fall 1997, p. 21.

CHAPTER IV
THE LAW AND POLITY: LEGISLATING MORALITY

1. Daniel Patrick Moynihan, *Miles to Go: A Personal History of Social Policy* (Cambridge, Mass., 1996), p. 63.
2. Thomas Paine, *Common Sense* (1776), in *Writings of Thomas Paine*, ed. Moncur Daniel Conway (New York, 1967), I, 69.
3. Edmund Burke, *Reflections on the Revolution in France* (1790) (Dolphin ed., New York, 1961), p. 72.
4. Ibid., p. 110. The paragraph in which this statement appears opens with a reference to "society," but then shifts to the "state." The antecedent of "it" in "It is a partnership . . ." is clearly "state." Moreover, "state" appears again in the sentence immediately following this. The misquotation appears in reference works as well as scholarly books: e.g., *A New Dictionary of Quotations on Historical Principles from Ancient and Modern Sources*, ed. H. L. Mencken (New York, 1962), p. 1120; *The Oxford Dictionary of Political Quotations*, ed. Antony Jay (Oxford, 1996), p. 67.
5. John Stuart Mill, *Representative Government* (1861) (Everyman ed., London, 1940), p. 193.

6. John Locke, *Two Treatises of Government* (1689), ed. Peter Laslett (2d ed., Cambridge, Eng., 1967), pp. 342–3 (*Second Treatise*, pars. 87–8).

7. Alexis de Tocqueville, *Democracy in America* (1835, 1840), ed. J. P. Mayer and Max Lerner, trans. George Lawrence (New York, 1966), pp. 174–180, 225, 492–3.

8. Ibid., pp. 224–5.

9. Ibid., pp. 492–3, 495.

10. Dan Coats, "The Project for American Renewal" (Washington, D.C., 1995). See *Policy Review*, Jan./Feb. 1996, pp. 24ff., for a summary of the Project and commentaries on it.

11. Quoted in Joe Loconte, "I'll Stand Bayou: Louisiana Couples Choose a More Muscular Marriage Contract," *Policy Review*, May/June 1998, p. 31.

12. James Q. Wilson and George L. Kelling, "Broken Windows," *Atlantic Monthly*, March 1982 (reprinted in Wilson, *On Character* [AEI Press, Washington, D.C., 1991], pp. 123–38).

13. John J. DiIulio, Jr., "Broken Bottles: Alcohol, Disorder, and Crime," *Brookings Review*, Spring 1996, pp. 14–17.

14. George Will, *The Woven Figure: Conservatism and America's Fabric, 1994–1997* (New York, 1997), p. 97.

15. *New York Times*, Jan. 19, 1998, p. A10. Another *Times* headline, several months later, reads: "Prison Population Growing Although Crime Rate Drops" (Aug. 8, 1998, p. A18).

16. Niccolò Machiavelli, *Political Discourses* (1531), in *The Works of Nicholas Machiavel*, trans. Ellis Farneworth (London, 1762), II, 56 (bk. I, chap. 18).

17. Thomas Hobbes, *Leviathan* (1651) (Everyman ed., London, 1943), p. 49.

18. Edmund Burke, "Letters on a Regicide Peace" (1796), in *The Works of Edmund Burke* (London, 1909–12), V, 208.

19. Edmund Burke, "A Letter to a Member of the National Assembly" (Jan. 19, 1791), in ibid., II, 555.

20. See, for example, Philip Howard, *The Death of Common Sense: How Law Is Suffocating America* (New York, 1994); Mary Ann Glendon, *A Nation Under Lawyers: How the Crisis in the Legal Profession Is Transforming American Society* (New York, 1994).

21. Robert H. Bork, "Our Judicial Oligarchy," *First Things*, Nov. 1996, pp. 21–4. See also Bork, *The Tempting of America: The Political Seduction of the Law* (New York, 1990), and *Slouching Towards Gomorrah: Modern Liberalism and American Decline* (New York,

1996). See also Max Boot, *Out of Order: Arrogance, Corruption, and Incompetence on the Bench* (New York, 1998).

22. *First Things*, Nov. 1996, p. 18.

23. Gertrude Himmelfarb, "On the Future of Conservatism," in *The End of Democracy? The Judicial Usurpation of Politics*, ed. Mitchell S. Muncy (Dallas, 1997), and the other essays in this volume.

24. *The State of Disunion: 1996 Survey of American Political Culture*, ed. James Davison Hunter and Carl Bowman (3 vols., Ivy, Va., 1996), I, 21. On the increasing dissatisfaction with the federal government, see Everett Carll Ladd and Karlyn Bowman, *What's Wrong: A Survey of Satisfaction and Complaint* (AEI Press, Washington, D.C., 1998), pp. 96–7.

25. The "real Washington bureaucracy," it has been said, has always resided not in Washington but in the states and localities that administer the programs Washington funds, and, as often as not, do so no more efficiently or responsibly than Washington itself. (William J. Bennett and John J. DiIulio, Jr., "What Good Is Government," *Commentary*, Nov. 1997, pp. 28–9.)

26. Franklin D. Roosevelt, Annual Message to Congress, Jan. 4, 1935, in *The Public Papers and Addresses of Franklin D. Roosevelt*, ed. Samuel I. Rosenman (New York, 1938), IV, 19–20.

27. *RFK: Collected Speeches*, ed. Edwin O. Guthman and C. Richard Allen (New York, 1993), pp. 209–10 (Feb. 7, 1966). (I am indebted to Michael Knox Beran, *The Last Patrician: Bobby Kennedy and the End of American Aristocracy* [New York, 1998], p. 106, for directing me to this source.)

28. "Aid to Families with Dependent Children and Temporary Assistance," updated Aug. 1998, Administration for Children and Families, U.S. Department of Health and Human Services.

29. *New York Times*, Jan. 21, 1998, p. A13 (citing President's Council of Economic Advisers).

30. *Washington Times*, Sept. 12, 1997, p. A22 (citing the New Jersey Department of Human Services and a Rutgers University study).

31. *New York Times*, Aug. 22, 1996, p. B1.

32. *RFK: Collected Speeches*, p. 188 (Dec. 10, 1966).

33. Lawrence M. Mead, "Telling the Poor What To Do," *Public Interest*, Summer 1998, pp. 97–112.

34. Charles Murray, "The Perils of GOP Activism," *Wall Street Journal*, Feb. 20, 1998, p. A18.

35. Carl E. Schneider, "The Law and the Stability of Marriage: The Family as a Social Institution," in *Promises to Keep: Decline*

and Renewal of Marriage in America, ed. David Popenoe, Jean Bethke Elshtain, and David Blankenhorn (Lanham, Md., 1996), pp. 201–2.

36. James L. Nolan, Jr., *The Therapeutic State: Justifying Government at Century's End* (New York, 1998).

37. Hannah Arendt, *The Human Condition* (Chicago, 1958), p. 23.

38. *The Basic Works of Aristotle,* ed. Richard McKeon (New York, 1941), p. 1129 (*Politics,* Bk. I, chap. 2).

39. Ibid., p. 1182 (Bk. III, chap. 4).

40. Charles Louis de Secondat, baron de Montesquieu, *The Spirit of the Laws,* trans. Thomas Nugent (New York, 1949), p. lxxi (Montesquieu's "Explanatory Notes").

41. Shirley Robin Letwin, *The Anatomy of Thatcherism* (London, 1992), pp. 35–6 and passim; David Brooks, "'Civil Society' and Its Discontents," *The Weekly Standard,* Feb. 5, 1996, pp. 18–21.

42. Bill Bradley, "America's Challenge: Revitalizing Our National Community," in *Community Works: The Revival of Civil Society in America,* ed. E. J. Dionne Jr. (Brookings Institution Press, Washington, D.C., 1998), p. 114.

43. *Wall Street Journal,* April 21, 1998, p. A24.

44. Georg Wilhelm Friedrich Hegel, *Philosophy of Right,* trans. and ed. T. M. Knox (Oxford, 1952), p. 267 (add. 116 to par. 182).

45. George F. Will, *Statecraft as Soulcraft: What Government Does* (New York, 1983).

46. Burke, *Reflections on the Revolution in France,* p. 59.

47. Ibid., pp. 213–14.

CHAPTER V

RELIGION: "THE FIRST OF THEIR POLITICAL INSTITUTIONS"

1. Jonathan Elliot, ed., *The Debates in the Several State Conventions, on the Adoption of the Federal Constitution* (Philadelphia, 1907), III, 536–7.

2. William Cabell Bruce, *Ben Franklin Self-Revealed* (New York, 1917), p. 90.

3. *The Works of John Adams* (Boston, 1854), IX, 229 (Letter to Officers of First Regiment, Oct. 11, 1798).

4. *The Writings of George Washington, 1744–1799,* ed. John C. Fitzpatrick (U.S. Government Printing Office, Washington, D.C., 1940), XXXV, 229.

5. Nicholas Von Hoffman, "God Was Present at the Founding,"

Civilization, April/May 1998, p. 39. (I have introduced quotation marks and paragraphing.)

6. Alexis de Tocqueville, *Democracy in America*, ed. J. P. Mayer and Max Lerner, trans. George Lawrence (New York, 1966), p. 477.

7. Ibid., pp. 271–2.

8. Ibid., p. 269.

9. Ibid.

10. Ibid., p. 40.

11. Ibid., p. 271.

12. Ibid., p. 269.

13. Ibid., p. 517.

14. On this aspect of Methodism, see Robert F. Wearmouth, *Methodism and the Common People of the Eighteenth Century* (London, 1945); Bernard Semmel, *The Methodist Revolution* (New York, 1973); Gertrude Himmelfarb, *The Idea of Poverty: England in the Early Industrial Age* (New York, 1983), pp. 31–5.

15. See the introductory essay to *The Evangelical Tradition in America*, ed. Leonard I. Sweet (Macon, Ga., 1984), for a bibliographical survey of this literature.

16. Martin E. Marty, *Religion, Awakening and Revolution* (Wilmington, N.C., 1977), p. 130.

17. Gordon Wood, *The Radicalism of the American Revolution* (New York, 1992), p. 331; Wood, "America's Unending Revolution," *Wilson Quarterly*, Spring 1999, p. 46.

18. Nathan O. Hatch, *The Democratization of American Christianity* (New Haven, 1989), pp. 4–5.

19. Robert W. Fogel, *The Fourth Great Awakening and the Future of Egalitarianism* (forthcoming, Chicago, 2000), appendix 1.1. See also Fogel, "The Fourth Great Awakening," *Wall Street Journal*, Jan. 9, 1996, p. A14. Fogel has a somewhat more schematic view of the Awakenings than most historians, drawing a closer connection between the theological aspect of each revival and its political and social ramifications.

20. *The State of Disunion: 1996 Survey of American Political Culture*, ed. James Davison Hunter and Carl Bowman (3 vols.; Ivy, Va., 1996), I, 52. (For the definition of "evangelical" used in this study, see p. 98, n. 13.)

21. One poll has 17 percent of the public describing themselves as "either a fundamentalist or an evangelical Christian." (*Wall Street Journal*/NBC News poll, Feb.–March 1998). Six months earlier, a

similar poll had 16 percent falling into that category (*Wall Street Journal*/NBC News poll, Sept. 1997). A more elaborate study, using a much more demanding definition of evangelicalism, has 20 million Americans identifying themselves as such. (Christian Smith, *American Evangelicalism: Embattled and Thriving* [Chicago, 1998], p. 1. For this definition of evangelicalism, see pp. 21–2.) A still more rigorous definition (based on nine theological criteria) has 12 million adults, or 6 percent of the population, failing into the category of evangelicals. The same survey, however, finds as many as 43 percent of adults, and 34 percent of teenagers, to be "born again" Christians. (Barna Research Group, Jan. 1998.)

22. CNN/*USA Today*/Gallup Poll, Jan. 1998.
23. Ralph E. Reed, Jr., "What Do Religious Conservatives Really Want?," in *Disciples and Democracy: Religious Conservatives and the Future of American Politics*, ed. Michael Cromartie (Grand Rapids, Mich., 1994), p. 2. See also Reed, *Politically Incorrect: The Emerging Faith Factor in American Politics* (Dallas, 1994).
24. George H. Gallup, Jr., *Religion in America 1996* (Princeton, 1996), p. 46.
25. *State of Disunion*, I, 52. In still another poll, half of the respondents (not only evangelicals) describe themselves as "theologically conservative," but only half of these identify themselves with the religious right. (Barna Research Group, Jan. 1998.)
26. *State of Disunion*, I, 53.
27. *Wall Street Journal*, Nov. 5, 1998, p. A22; *Washington Post*, Nov. 5, 1998, p. A34.
28. Smith, pp. 75–84.
29. Gallup, pp. 52–3.
30. Stephen L. Carter, *The Dissent of the Governed: A Meditation on Law, Religion, and Loyalty* (Cambridge, Mass., 1998), p. 9.
31. Russell Shorto, "Belief by the Numbers," *New York Times Magazine*, Dec. 7, 1997, p. 61 (citing Roper report).
32. Marshall W. Fishwick, *Great Awakenings: Popular Religion and Popular Culture* (New York, 1995), p. 13.
33. "Tocqueville and the Mullah," *The New Republic*, Feb. 2, 1998, p. 7.
34. David Martin, *Tongues of Fire: The Explosion of Protestantism in Latin America* (Oxford, 1990), pp. 50–52.
35. *Washington Post*, Jan. 24, 1999, p. A19.
36. George H. Gallup, Jr., *Religion in America 1992–93* (Princeton, 1993), p. 70. The CNN/*USA Today*/Gallup Poll for Jan. 1998 has

58 percent of Americans saying that religion is very important in their lives.

37. *New York Times*, Sept. 6, 1997, p. A14.

38. Václav Havel, "Faith in the World," *Civilization*, April/May 1998, p. 53.

39. Roger Finke and Rodney Stark, *The Churching of America, 1776–1990* (New Brunswick, N.J., 1994). Some commentators on "American exceptionalism" manage to discuss the subject without any reference to religion (e.g., Ian Tyrrell, "American Exceptionalism in an Age of International History," *American Historical Review*, Oct. 1991; Michael Kammen, "The Problem of American Exceptionalism: A Reconsideration," *American Quarterly*, March 1993).

40. Gallup, *Religion in America 1996*, pp. 22, 4–5, 37. I have updated some of these figures in accord with the CNN/*USA Today*/Gallup Poll of Jan. 1998, and the *Washington Post*/Kaiser Family Foundation/Harvard University poll of July–Aug. 1998.

41. Shorto, p. 61.

42. For a criticism of the polls on this subject, see C. Kirk Hadaway, Penny Long Marler, and Mark Chaves, "What the Polls Don't Show: A Closer Look at U.S. Church Attendance," *American Sociological Review*, 1993; Guenter Lewy, *Why America Needs Religion: Secular Modernity and Its Discontents* (Grand Rapids, Mich., 1996), p. 68.

43. Barna Research Group, Jan. 1998.

44. These findings have been amply documented. See the extensive bibliography cited in "Testimony concerning the Effects of Stress, Relaxation, and Belief on Health and Healthcare Costs" by Harold G. Koenig to the U.S. Senate Appropriations Subcommittee on Labor/HHS and Education, Sept. 22, 1998, pp. 7–9. See also *Why Religion Matters: The Impact of Religious Practice on Social Stability* (Heritage Foundation, Jan. 1996), and publications from the Center for the Study of Religion/Spirituality and Health at the Duke University Medical Center.

45. CNN/*USA Today*/Gallup Poll, Apr.–May 1999.

46. Tocqueville, p. 267.

47. Diane Winston, "Campuses Are a Bellwether for Society's Religious Revival," *Chronicle of Higher Education*, Jan. 16, 1998, p. A60. On similarly syncretic tendencies outside the campus, see *Wall Street Journal*, Feb. 10, 1999, pp. B1–2.

48. Shorto, p. 60.

49. Gallup, *Religion in America 1996,* p. 9.
50. James Davison Hunter, "The Evangelical Worldview Since 1890," in *Piety and Politics: Evangelicals and Fundamentalists Confront the World,* ed. Richard John Neuhaus and Michael Cromartie (Ethics and Public Policy Center, Washington, D.C., 1987), p. 45.
51. Robert Wuthnow, *The Restructuring of American Religion: Society and Faith Since World War II* (Princeton, 1988), pp. 132 ff. See also James Davison Hunter, *Culture Wars: The Struggle to Define America* (New York, 1991); Nancy T. Ammerman, *Baptist Battles: Social Change and Religious Conflict in the Southern Baptist Convention* (New Brunswick, N.J., 1990).
52. David F. Wells, *Losing Our Virtue: Why the Church Must Recover Its Moral Vision* (Grand Rapids, Mich., 1998). See also Hunter on the differences among evangelicals in *Partisan Review,* Spring 1997, pp. 187–96.
53. Shorto, p. 61.
54. Hunter, *Culture Wars,* p. 47.
55. John C. Green, Lyman A. Kellstedt, Corwin E. Smidt, and James L. Guth, "Who Elected Clinton: A Collision of Values," *First Things,* Aug./Sept. 1997, p. 35; and the same authors in "The Political Relevance of Religion," in *Religion and the Culture Wars: Dispatches from the Front,* ed. by the above (Lanham, Md., 1996), p. 323. See also Fred Barnes, "The Orthodox Alliance," *American Enterprise,* Nov./Dec. 1995, p. 70.
56. George Marsden, "The Evangelical Denomination," in *Piety and Politics,* p. 55.
57. "Evangelicals and Catholics Together: The Christian Mission in the Third Millennium," *First Things,* May 1994, pp. 15–22. This sense of fraternity was somewhat disrupted when the Pope, in his visit to Mexico in January 1999, referred to non-Catholic churches as "sects."
58. Sherwood Eliot Wirt, *The Social Conscience of the Evangelical* (New York, 1968), p. 92.
59. Everett Carll Ladd, *The Ladd Report* (New York, 1999), p. 47 (citing *Yearbook of American and Canadian Churches,* 1962 and 1997).
60. Stephen L. Carter, *The Culture of Disbelief: How American Law and Politics Trivialize Religious Devotion* (New York, 1993), p. 8. See also Jean Bethke Elshtain, "The Bright Line: Liberalism and Religion," *New Criterion,* March 1999.

61. Michael Weisskopf, "Energized by Pulpit or Passion," *Washington Post*, Feb. 1, 1993, p. A1.

62. On the Promise Keepers, see *The Public Perspective*, Dec./Jan. 1998, p. 14. On the Christian Right, see *State of Disunion*, I, 53–5.

63. *State of Disunion*, I, 60–1.

64. Peter Berger, *A Far Glory: Safe in an Age of Credulity* (New York, 1991); Berger, "Secularism in Retreat," *National Interest*, Winter 1996/97.

65. Amitai Etzioni, *The Spirit of Community: Rights, Responsibilities, and the Communitarian Agenda* (New York, 1993), p. 53.

66. Alan Wolfe, *Whose Keeper? Social Science and Moral Obligation* (Berkeley, 1989), p. 3. In support of this statement, Wolfe cites the disagreements within the mainline churches, but he does not mention the evangelical churches, Mormons, or the religious revival in general.

67. Richard T. Gill, *Posterity Lost: Progress, Ideology, and the Decline of the American Family* (Lanham, Md., 1997), p. 302.

68. Michael Sandel, *Democracy's Discontent: America in Search of a Public Philosophy* (Cambridge, Mass., 1996), pp. 55ff, 309, 328. There is no reference in the index to churches, evangelicalism, the religious revival, or any specific religious denomination.

69. Christopher Lasch, *Haven in a Heartless World* (New York, 1977), p. 228.

70. Michael Kazin, "The Politics of Devotion," *The Nation*, April 6, 1998, pp. 16–19.

71. Alan Brinkley, *Liberalism and Its Discontents* (Cambridge, Mass., 1998), pp. 295–6.

72. Robert N. Bellah, *The Broken Covenant: American Civil Religion in Time of Trial* (2d ed., Chicago, 1992 [1st ed., 1975]), p. 135. See also Bellah, "Civil Religion in America," *Daedalus*, Winter 1967, and "Religion and the Legitimation of the American Republic," in *Varieties of Civil Religion*, ed. Phillip E. Hammond and Robert Bellah (New York, 1980).

73. Bellah, *Broken Covenant* (2d ed.), p. x. In his more popular book, *Habits of the Heart* (Berkeley, 1985), the term does not appear. More recently, Bellah has urged a greater respect for traditional religion, rebuking those secularists who want to "get rid of religion altogether." The danger, he said, came less from the religious right than from "a loosely bounded culture which, were it ever completely successful, would destroy both the moral norms

that provide the terms for our democratic conversation and the communities that carry those moral norms and ethical concerns, including the religious communities." ("Conclusion: Competing Visions of the Role of Religion in American Society," in *Uncivil Religion: Interreligious Hostility in America*, ed. Robert N. Bellah and Frederick E. Greenspahn [New York, 1987], pp. 220, 231.)

74. Jean-Jacques Rousseau, *The Social Contract* (New York, n.d.), pp. 110–15 (Bk. IV, ch. 8).

75. Carol Blum, *Rousseau and the Republic of Virtue: The Language of Politics in the French Revolution* (Ithaca, 1986), pp. 235–6.

76. Sanford Kessler, *Tocqueville's Civil Religion: American Christianity and the Prospects for Freedom* (Albany, 1994).

77. Emile Durkheim, *The Elementary Forms of the Religious Life: A Study in Religious Sociology*, trans. Joseph Ward Swain (Glencoe, Ill., 1947 [1st Fr. ed., 1912]), pp. 427, 419.

78. *Newsweek*, Oct. 25, 1976, p. 68.

79. Richard John Neuhaus, "From Civil Religion to Public Philosophy," in *Civil Religion and Political Theology*, ed. Leroy S. Roumer (Notre Dame, 1986), p. 99.

80. John J. DiIulio, Jr., "The World's Work: The Church and the 'Civil Society Sector,'" *Brookings Review*, Fall 1997, p. 28. See also Joe Klein, "Can Faith-Based Groups Save Us," *The Responsive Community*, Winter 1997/98.

81. Eugene F. Rivers III, "High Octane Faith and Civil Society," in *Community Works: The Revival of Civil Society in America* (Brookings Institution Press, Washington, D.C., 1998), p. 61; *Washington Post*, Oct. 23, 1997, p. A3.

82. Joe Loconte, "Making Criminals Pay: A New York County's Bold Experiment in Biblical Justice," *Policy Review*, Jan./Feb. 1998, pp. 26–31.

83. Joe Loconte, "Jailhouse Rock of Ages," *Policy Review*, July/Aug. 1997, pp. 12–14.

84. Tucker Carlson, "Deliver Us From Evil: Prison Fellowship's Saving Grace," in *Making America Safer*, ed. Edwin Meese III and Robert E. Moffitt (Heritage Foundation, Washington, D.C., 1997), p. 200. (Originally published in *Policy Review*, Fall 1992, the essay was updated by Kim Robbins in March 1997.)

85. Stuart M. Butler, "Practical Principles," in *To Empower People: From State to Civil Society*, ed. Peter L. Berger and Richard John

Neuhaus, 2d ed., ed. Michael Novak (AEI Press, Washington, D.C., 1996), p. 119. See also Woodson's essay in the same volume, "Success Stories," pp. 105–15.

86. DiIulio, *Brookings Review*, Fall 1997, p. 29.

87. Robert L. Woodson, Sr., "Can Faith-Based Groups Save Us?" *The Responsive Community*, Winter 1997/98, p. 48.

88. Louis M. Nanni, *American Enterprise*, Jan./Feb. 1995, p. 60. See also Marvin Olasky, "The Corruption of Religious Charities," in *To Empower People*, pp. 94–104; Glenn C. Loury and Linda Datcher Loury, "Not By Bread Alone: The Role of the African-American Church in Inner-City Development," *Brookings Review*, Winter 1997, pp. 10–13; Amy Sherman, *Restorers of Hope* (Wheaton, Ill., 1997).

89. Carter, *The Culture of Disbelief*. See also Joe Loconte, "The Bully and the Pulpit: A New Model for Church-State Partnerships," *Policy Review*, Nov./Dec. 1998, pp. 28–37.

90. Statement issued by the mayor's office on the city's program, the "Front Porch Alliance."

91. Herbert H. Toler, Jr., "Fisher of Men: A Baltimore Minister Promotes Black Christian Manhood," *Policy Review*, Spring 1995, p. 70.

92. *Wall Street Journal*, Aug. 20, 1998, p. A15.

93. Carter, *Culture of Disbelief*, p. 40.

94. Smith, p. 117 and passim.

95. Richard John Neuhaus, "What the Fundamentalists Want," in *Piety and Politics: Evangelicals and Fundamentalists Confront the World*, ed. Neuhaus and Michael Cromartie (Ethics and Public Policy Center, Washington, D.C., 1987), p. 14.

96. Timothy George, "Southern Baptist Ghosts," *First Things*, May 1999, p. 24.

97. A. James Reichley, "The Evangelical and Fundamentalist Revolt," in *Piety and Politics*, p. 89.

98. Peter Beinart, "The Big Debate," *New Republic*, March 16, 1998, p. 22.

99. Nathan Glazer, "Fundamentalists: A Defensive Offensive," in *Piety and Politics*, pp. 245–58.

100. Stephen Carter, *The Dissent of the Governed: A Meditation on Law, Religion, and Loyalty* (Cambridge, Mass., 1998).

101. *The Works of the Right Honourable Edmund Burke* (Oxford [World's Classics ed.], 1930), pp. 187–8.

102. Matthew Arnold, *Culture and Anarchy*, ed. J. Dover Wilson (Cambridge, Eng., 1957), p. 56.

CHAPTER VI

THE TWO CULTURES: "AN ETHICS GAP"

1. *Public Perspective* (Roper Center), June/July 1998, pp. 23–7.
2. Ralph Reed, *Active Faith: How Christians Are Changing the Soul of American Politics* (New York, 1996), pp. 220–4.
3. *Washington Post*, Sept. 26, 1997, p. A25.
4. *Public Perspective*, Dec./Jan. 1998, p. 32 (citing Gallup poll, Aug. 1997); *What's Happening to Abortion Rates?* (Sexuality and American Social Policy, Kaiser Foundation, 1996), p. 54; Robert Lerner, Althea K. Nagai, and Stanley Rothman, *American Elites* (New Haven, 1996), p. 91.
5. Stephen Powers, David J. Rothman, and Stanley Rothman, *Hollywood's America: Social and Political Themes in Motion Pictures* (Boulder, Colo., 1996), p. 74; Lerner et al., *American Elites*, p. 91; Gallup Poll, June 10, 1997; *Time*/CNN poll, June–July 1998.
6. George H. Gallup, Jr., *Religion in America 1996* (Princeton, 1996), p. 30; Powers et al., *Hollywood's America*, p. 54.
7. *Chronicle of Higher Education*, Nov. 7, 1997, p. A14.
8. Mary Ann Lamanna and Agnes Riedmann, *Marriages and Families: Making Choices in a Diverse Society* (6th ed., Belmont, Calif., 1997), pp. 4–5.
9. Richard T. Gill, *Posterity Lost: Progress, Ideology, and the Decline of the American Family* (Lanham, Md., 1997), p. 257. The 1992 edition of *The American Heritage Dictionary* dropped the words "blood, marriage, or adoption" from its definition of family and substituted "two or more people who share goals or values, have long-term commitment to one another, and reside usually in the same dwelling place." (Cited by Barbara Dafoe Whitehead, in "For As Long as We Both Shall Like," *New Republic*, July/Aug. 1997.)
10. *Wall Street Journal*/NBC News poll, March 1998; *Washington Post*/Kaiser Foundation/Harvard University poll, Jul.–Aug. 1998.
11. *Time*/CNN poll, June–July 1998. Reports of those who "personally know" others who have committed adultery are in striking variance with those who themselves admit to having committed adultery. In a 1994 poll conducted by the National Opinion Research Center at the University of Chicago, only 21 percent of men and 11 percent of women say they committed adultery at some point in their marriage—this compared with the 70 percent of men and 60 percent of women who are "known" to have done

so. It is entirely probable that people underestimate their own adulterous affairs and overestimate those of others.

12. Robert L. Simon, "The Paralysis of 'Absolutophobia'," *Chronicle of Higher Education*, June 27, 1997, p. B5.

13. James Q. Wilson, *The Moral Sense* (New York, 1993), p. 8.

14. Kay Haugaard, "Students Who Won't Decry Evil—A Case of Too Much Tolerance," *Chronicle of Higher Education*, June 27, 1997, p. B4.

15. See notes 9 and 10 above.

16. Nathan O. Hatch, *The Democratization of American Christianity* (New Haven, 1989), pp. 218–19.

17. *The State of Disunion: 1996 Survey of American Political Culture*, ed. James Davison Hunter and Carl Bowman (3 vols.; Ivy, Va., 1996), I, 86–9.

18. *Wall Street Journal*, Oct. 16, 1997, p. A1. (The game is "Postal.")

19. For example, the video game "Doom" and the movie *The Basketball Diaries*.

20. Terrence McNally's *Corpus Christi*.

21. Jane Gallop, of the University of Wisconsin. (See Gertrude Himmelfarb, "Professor Narcissus," *Weekly Standard*, June 2, 1997.)

22. *New York Times*, July 16, 1997, p. C18. See also *Times*, Nov. 16, 1997, Arts section, p. 41.

23. Caryn James, "Straying into Temptation in Prime Time," *New York Times*, Aug. 10, 1997, Arts section, pp. 1, 32. See also *Sex and Hollywood: Should There Be a Government Role?* (Sexuality and American Social Policy, Kaiser Foundation, 1996), p. xiii.

24. *New York Times*, April 6, 1998, p. A1.

25. *New York Times*, April 17, 1998, p. A16.

26. *New York Times*, August 2, 1998, Week in Review section, p. 2; *Public Perspective,* Feb./March 1998, p. 21.

27. *New York Times,* March 21, 1999, "Style" section, p. 1; ibid., March 27, 1999, p. A22.

28. American Council on Education, UCLA, 1998.

29. *Chronicle of Higher Education*, Nov. 30, 1994, p. A30; Sept. 19, 1997, pp. B4–5; Jan. 16, 1998, p. A60.

30. *New York Times*/CBS News poll, April 30, 1998; "Gallup Youth Report," Nov. 1996, p. 3.

31. *New York Times*, April 30, 1998, p. A1; Frederica Mathewes-Green, "Now for Some Good News," *First Things*, Aug./Sept. 1997, p. 21.

32. Edward O. Laumann, John H. Gagnon, Robert T. Michael, and

Stuart Michaels, *The Social Organization of Sexuality: Sexual Practices in the United States* (Chicago, 1994), p. 543.

33. *American Enterprise*, July/Aug. 1995, p. 103 (citing Opinion Research Center, 1994); ibid., Jan./Feb. 1998, p. 93 (citing Opinion Research Center, 1996); *Wall Street Journal*/NBC News poll, Feb.–March 1998; *Washington Post*/Kaiser Family Foundation/Harvard University poll, July–Aug. 1998.

34. *New York Times*, Oct. 1, 1997, p. A24; *Forward*, Aug. 29, 1997, p. 3; ibid., Jan. 23, 1998, pp. 1–2; ibid., March 27, 1998, pp. 1, 5.

35. *Chronicle of Higher Education,* March 5, 1999, p. A42. See also *New York Times,* Aug. 26, 1998, p. A20.

36. National Home Education Research Institute Report, March 1997; Katherine Pfleger, "School's Out," *New Republic*, April 6, 1998, p. 11; *Chronicle of Higher Education*, July 18, 1997, p. A34; *Economist*, June 6, 1998, pp. 28–9; *Washington Post*, April 24, 1998, pp. A1, 16; *Investor's Business Daily*, March 29, 1999, p. 1 (citing Education Policy Analysis Archives).

37. *American Enterprise*, Sept./Oct. 1997, p. 63.

38. *Chronicle of Higher Education*, Sept. 18, 1998, p. A49 (citing *Journal of American College Health*, Sept. 1998).

39. Richard Miniter, "America's Newest Corporate Address Is Home Sweet Home," *American Enterprise*, May/June 1998, p. 52.

40. Margaret Talbot, "Getting Credit for Being White," *New York Times Magazine*, Nov. 30, 1997, p. 116.

41. *American Enterprise*, Sept./Oct. 1997, p. 5.

42. Christian Smith and David Sikking, "Is Private School Privatizing?," *First Things,* April 1999, pp. 16–20 (citing National Household Education Survey of the Department of Education, 1996).

43. *Washington Post*, Feb. 18, 1999, p. A6; *New York Times*, Feb. 21, 1999, p. WK3; *Washington Post,* March 7, 1999, p. B7.

44. *State of Disunion*, I, 55–6.

45. Alan Wolfe, *One Nation, After All: What Middle-Class Americans Really Think About God/Country/Family/Racism/Welfare/Immigration/Homosexuality/Work/The Right/The Left/and Each Other* (New York, 1998). In an interview with David Gergen on the Lehrer Newshour (March 11, 1998), Wolfe prided himself on having actually "gone out and talked to the American people," unlike, he said, many people who speak about the "culture war." He talked to a total of 200 people in eight suburban middle-class communities, for one to one-and-a-half hours each. This compares with *The State of Disunion*, which is based upon a Gallup survey ten

times that size, in which 2,000 people were interviewed for an hour or more each.

46. Wolfe, *One Nation*, pp. 47, 102.

47. Ibid., pp. 49, 71.

48. American Jewish Committee, *A Survey of the Religious Right* (New York, 1996), p. 8. This survey was conducted between May 10 and June 3, 1996. Wolfe does not give any dates for his survey, but it must have been about the same time as this or shortly afterward.

49. Wolfe, *One Nation*, pp. 70–1.

50. Alan Wolfe, *Whose Keeper? Social Science and Moral Obligation* (Berkeley, 1989), pp. 3–7.

51. Gergen interview, March 11, 1998.

52. Wolfe, *One Nation* , p. 76.

53. Ibid., p. 276.

54. Ibid., pp. 54, 291.

55. See p. 125 above.

56. James Davison Hunter, *Culture Wars: The Struggle to Define America* (New York, 1991), pp. 107, 128, and passim.

57. Hunter, "The American Culture War," in *The Limits of Social Cohesion: Conflict and Mediation in Pluralist Societies*, ed. Peter L. Berger (New York, 1998), pp. 2–14.

58. George Weigel, "Talking the Talk: Christian Conviction and Democratic Etiquette," in *Disciples and Democracy: Religious Conservatives and the Future of American Politics*, ed. Michael Cromartie (Grand Rapids, Mich., 1994), pp. 90–4.

59. Peter L. Berger, "Conclusion: General Observations on Normative Conflicts and Mediation," in *The Limits of Social Cohesion,* p. 355.

60. Ibid., pp. 355–6.

61. Michael Walzer, *On Toleration* (New Haven, 1997), pp. 10–11. See also Adam Wolfson, "What Remains of Toleration," *Public Interest*, Winter 1999.

62. *Washington Post*/Kaiser Family Foundation/Harvard University poll, Aug. 16 and 27, 1998.

63. Walzer, p. 66.

64. *Washington Post*/Kaiser Family Foundation/Harvard University poll, Aug. 27, 1998.

EPILOGUE: SOME MODEST PREDICTIONS

1. Sean Wilentz, "God and Man at Lynchburg," *New Republic*, Apr. 25, 1988, p. 30.
2. *Washington Post*, June 12, 1989, p. A11.
3. See p. 113 for Richard Neuhaus's comment on the "magnificently fissiparous" nature of fundamentalism.
4. Robert W. Fogel comes close to this in "The Fourth Great Awakening," *Wall Street Journal*, Jan. 9, 1996, p. A14.
5. Jerry Falwell, "Moral Majority a Reaction to Attack on Basic Values of Millions of Americans," *Conservative Digest*, Jan. 1981, p. 28. See also James L. Guth, "The Politics of the Christian Right," in *Religion and the Culture Wars: Dispatches from the Front,* ed. James L. Guth, John C. Green, Corwin E. Smidt, and Lyman Kellstedt (Lanham, Md., 1996), p. 15.

INDEX

A NOTE ABOUT THE AUTHOR

Gertrude Himmelfarb was born in New York City, received her bachelor's degree from Brooklyn College, and went on to the University of Chicago for her master's and doctorate. She taught at the Graduate School of the City University of New York, where she was named Distinguished Professor of History in 1978. Now Professor Emeritus, she lives with her husband, Irving Kristol, in Washington, D.C. The National Council on the Humanities named her the 1991 Jefferson Lecturer, the highest honor the federal government bestows for distinguished achievement in the humanities. In 1997 she received the Templeton Award for *The De-Moralization of Society.*

A NOTE ON THE TYPE

The text of this book was set in a digitized version of Bembo, a well-known Monotype face. Named for Pietro Bembo, the celebrated Renaissance writer and humanist scholar who was made a cardinal and served as secretary to Pope Leo X, the original cutting of Bembo was made by Francesco Griffo of Bologna only a few years after Columbus discovered America.

Composed by NK Graphics, Keene, New Hampshire

Printed and bound by Haddon Craftsmen,
Bloomsburg, Pennsylvania

Designed by Dorothy S. Baker